By the same author

Fiction

A Far Cry from Clammergoose
High Walk to Wandlemere
Ravens in Winter

Non Fiction

Discovering the Isle of Wight
Villages of the Isle of Wight
Discovering the New Forest
A Watcher in the Woods
Walking on the Isle of Wight

Children's Fiction

Danger at Dark Howes
The Secret of Wanstone Wood

Caroline & Robert
A Laureate's Romance

Patricia Sibley

Hunnyhill Publications
1997

For permission to use original manuscripts -

HAMPSHIRE RECORD OFFICE for Mss.69-108. UNIVERSITY OF ROCHESTER LIBRARY, NEW YORK, for letters from ROBERT SOUTHEY PAPERS in the Dept of Rare Books and special collections. THE TRUSTEES OF THE NATIONAL LIBRARY OF SCOTLAND for use of their BLACKWOOD PAPERS. DR RAYMOND TURLEY, of the HARTLEY LIBRARY, UNIVERSITY OF SOUTHAMPTON. For much help in tracing C.B.'s printed books, TIM BLACKMORE A.L.A. HEAD OF LIBRARY SERVICES AND INFORMATION SERVICES, ISLE OF WIGHT COUNCIL CULTURAL SERVICES. Also to THE BRITISH LIBRARY, INDIA OFFICE LIBRARY, STATES OF JERSEY LIBRARY SERVICE, UNIVERSITY OF READING LIBRARY, SUSSEX RECORD OFFICE, THE ROYAL COMMISSION OF HISTORICAL MANUSCRIPTS, THE WORDSWORTH TRUST, DOVE COTTAGE GRASMERE and LONGMAN, PUBLISHERS. Also to G. SOUTHERN of ENGLISH HERITAGE, at CALSHOT CASTLE; WALHAMPTON SCHOOL, LYMINGTON; DAPHNE STONE; H.R. BOYCE and DR & Mrs IVOR JOHNSON of Buckland Cottage. To my Lymington friends GEORGE & SYLVIA HOLLOBONE, LIZ RUTTER, BARBARA WAKEFORD, the late TED MARSH. To ROBERT BARRETT B.A. And to my editor ELIZABETH HUTCHINGS for all her hard work and enthusiasm.

Other sources. THE CORRESPONDENCE OF ROBERT SOUTHEY WITH CAROLINE BOWLES, ed. Edward Dowden, 1881. CORRESPONDENCE WITH THE WORDSWORTH CIRCLE, Henry Crabb Robinson, 1935 Ed. Morley. ARTICLE IN CORNHILL MAGAZINE by E.O.

CHAPTERS

A Fair Place and Pleasant 1
A Whirl of Dissipation 18
A Bird from an Eastern Land 37
Dear and Kind Friend of Mine 47
A Little Bit of a VIrago 67
The Lion's Tail. 82
A Perfect Conformity of Disposition 97
We Came Together at Life's Eventide 119
All Here is Finished - Gloriously Restored 138

ILLUSTRATIONS
Between pages 74 & 75

Caroline Bowles Self Portrait
Courtesy of The Wordsworth Trust

Robert Southey by Henry Edridge 1769 -1821
Courtesy of The National Portrait Gallery London
Buckland Cottage Author
Courtesy of Dr Ivor Johnson
Greta Hall and Keswick Bridge by W. Westall
Courtesy of The Wordsworth Trust

© Patricia Sibley 1997

ISBN 0 9521939 3 0

British Library Cataloguing-in-Publication-Data.
A catalogue record for this book is available from the British Library

Published by Hunnyhill Publications
Corner Cottage Hunnyhill Brighstone Newport
Isle of Wight PO30 4DU
Tel: 01 983 740363

Printed by Hobbs the Printers Ltd, Totton, Hampshire SO40 3WX
from camera-ready copy supplied

chapter one

A fair place and pleasant

"This is a bitter night for the young lambs," said Charles Bowles, drawing his chair closer to the blazing logs, though careful not to disturb the elderly setter, Di, who slept at his feet.

Outside, snow whirled down on the New Forest and the pasture lands round Lymington: occasionally it ceased, only for hailstones to clatter down the windows, while great gusts of wind buffeted the house. The world outside might be stormy, England at war with revolutionary France, but inside Buckland Cottage all was peaceful and secure.

The family grouped about the fire hardly noticed an urgent knocking on the back door: a servant would see to it. Portraits of ancestors looked down from panelled walls on carved, mahogany furniture, bookcases, tall vases from India; damask curtains glowed a warm amber in the lamplight. Round the fire sat the old ladies and Anne, Charles' wife, stitching a tapestry. Caroline was drawing, perched high on a chair with a thick cushion atop a book so that she could reach the table, while Chloé, her spaniel, slept beneath. Caroline drew a coach and six horses, a house with many windows, confident of loving praise for her efforts, but presently dropped her pencil, slid to the floor, pulled up her own special stool and came to lean against her father's knees, an elfin, delicate-boned child with bright auburn curls.

"Cary, what makes you look so sad?" her mother asked.

Cary was worried about the lambs. Out with her father that afternoon, she had seen them in their hurdled pens, some hardly able to stand up. Would not such a bitter night kill the little things?

"Shepherd will take good care of them and God tempers the wind to the shorn lamb," her father said, looking up from his book. Just at that moment the door was opened by Joe, their manservant, and in came a huge, bear-like figure, cap and shaggy-bundled coat still white with snow.

"Why Farmer, whatever's the matter that you're out this wild night!" Charles exclaimed. "My daughter was only this minute worrying about your lambs."

Caroline had already run to her old friend, excited by the unexpected visit of this bruin-like figure and the promise of some special surprise in the knowing twinkle of his eyes.

"I'll lay my life Miss will never guess what I've got here all cuddled up so warm under my old coat, but it's for her." As well as the spaniel and her pony, Caroline had a whole menagerie of small creatures, rescued and adopted, whom she adored and her small face lit with joy when a new-born lamb was revealed. "I know Miss will mud it up clever as a little queen if I may leave it for her."

If ... the pause was fraught with awful suspense. Caroline looked from Father to Mother. Though both were smiling, they shook their heads, about to thank the farmer and say the lamb really could not stay, till she flew from one to the other, kissing and imploring. She was *their* one ewe lamb, late born, the chief joy of the old ladies too. So they gave in, and the lamb, christened Willy, became Caroline's inseparable companion.

This vignette of life at Buckland Cottage reveals many of the strands which would weave her life's tapestry, a loved and petted childhood, a deeply pious atmosphere, books and sketching, a strong love of animals, above all a household which revolved round her small person. All conspired to make this a time of idyllic happiness and security, which could never be equalled. Many writers in old age look back to their childhoods, but Caroline even in her twenties and thirties yearned back to the time when she had -

> Two parents then, inestimable wealth,
> Two parents, me, their only darling blessed.

Caroline Anne Bowles was born at Buckland on December 6th 1786. Charles Bowles did not become a father till he was forty eight, about the same time as he retired from the East India Company and moved into Buckland House on the outskirts of Lymington, Hampshire, renting it from a remote cousin of his wife's, John Bond, but soon buying smaller, homelier Buckland Cottage on the opposite side of the road. (There is said to be a smugglers' tunnel linking the two houses) Caroline was too small to remember the move - it seemed to her she had always lived at the cottage.

Charles had two sisters, Anne and Sara, an elder brother George, and another, Edward, who like their father, practised as a solicitor in Bartlett's Buildings, Holborn. Edward had five children, Caroline's first cousins, but on the whole her mother's relations, being nearer to hand, were to play the strongest parts in her life. The Bowles family included minor landed gentry - great grandfather had a large estate in Worcestershire - respected figures in the community, a Mayor, a High Sheriff, even an M.P. and a Brigadier General, whilst Charles himself was three times Mayor of Lymington.

Caroline pictures her father as a quiet, withdrawn and bookish figure who must be treated with care during frequent bouts of nervous depression - a rather sad and silent man. Years later she was to write, "I recollect the dreadful intervals of gloom that came upon him, lasting for weeks, for months and finally terminating in fits that wore away his mental power. I recollect too how often he used to look mournfully on me and say, 'My poor child, you resemble me too much in all things.'"

How this bright and wilful child must have lightened the elderly and ageing household of Buckland Cottage, as she grew older becoming a special companion to her father, and it was by no means all gloom.

Even before she could write, Caroline began to make up poems and stories of her own, which she would dictate to her father, wild rhapsodies about gardens and elves, silver streams and fleecy flocks. She never went to school so seldom saw other children. It was her father who taught her to write -

> Unsteady and perplexed the first attempts.
> Great A's that with colossal strides encroached
> On twice the space they should have occupied
> And sprawling V's and Y's
> Gaping prodigiously, like butterboats.

The great delight of father and daughter was to go fishing together along the flowery banks of Boldre Stream, the infant Lymington River, which ran through the valley below, a green and secret world overhung with willow and alder, bright in summer with purple loosestrife, comfrey and buttercups. While her father fished, Caroline performed the rites. First she took the picnic basket and stowed it away in the Naiad's Grot, a little cave in the bank beneath a rustic footbridge, then she would creep to her father's side, and without any word which might disturb the fish, take a book from his deep pocket and steal away to another special place further along the bank.

In her thirties, Caroline was to write a long autobiographical poem, *The Birthday*, describing her childhood in loving detail. While the view back may have become a little rose-tinted by then, the facts remain. This is her reading-place by Boldre Stream.

> Just where the river with graceful curve
> Darkened and deepened in the leafy gloom
> Of a huge pollard oak, a snug retreat
> I found me at the foot of that old tree,
> Within the grotto-work of its vast roots
> From whose fantastic arches, high upheaved,
> Sprang plumy clusters of the jewelled fern.

Here she was content for hours, reading Isaac Walton's *The Compleat Angler*, a strange book for a small girl to love so much, but totally fitting time and place, with its quaint directions on, '*How to fish for, and to dress, the* Chavender, *or* CHUB, and rid it of its watery humour.' Presently it was time to picnic, but this was no hasty affair of grabbing a sandwich. First, the most beautiful spot must be selected, often a clearing in the wood, carpeted with moss and wild strawberry: there a white cloth was spread, weighted down with a stone at each corner. When all was arranged to her precise liking, including the silver cups beside their respective flasks of cider and of milk, she would fetch her father. When they had eaten, and Father returned to his rod, the next ritual was to spread crumbs for the birds, and hide titbits among the branches overhead, for the red squirrels. In the long summer day she would return to her oak -

> Still as an image in its carved shrine
> I nestled in my sylvan niche, like hare
> Upgathered in her form,

content to watch robin or kingfisher or the trout in their water-world, knowing that her father's loving presence was never far away. She took his long silences for granted, sometimes returning to his side just to exchange a smile, wise beyond her years.

Anne Bowles, her mother, belonged to the well-known Burrard family, one branch of which had furnished Lymington with members of parliament for the last two hundred years and built a Queen Anne mansion on their four hundred acre estate, Walhampton, just across the Lymington River. This was now the home of Anne's cousin, Admiral Sir Harry Burrard. He was Commander-in-chief of the Mediterranean Fleet and a close friend of King George III who often stayed at Walhampton or sailed the Channel in Sir Harry's frigate. The family claimed a Norman ancestor, Guillame de Bosc Ruard, the latter part becoming gradually anglicised into Borrard and finally 'Hampshirised' into Burrard. Anne's brother Philip now worked for His Majesty's Customs in London, while another Sir Harry was a Lieutenant General and Governor of nearby Calshot Castle. Their mother, Madeleine Durrell, came of a proud Norman-speaking Jersey family, so Caroline grew up bi-lingual, learning French from her mother as early as English from the rest of the household.

For thirty years Caroline was to share a close and loving relationship with her mother. One of her earliest memories was searching the rambling cottage garden for wild, white violets for her, because they smelled sweeter than the cultivated ones. From her mother she learned laboriously to sew, hating dull seams which always got dirty before they were finished, but later she would spend many contented evenings sewing while her mother read aloud or told stories. In one of her own stories, *Broad Summerford*, Caroline was to look lovingly back at such times. "Those quiet hours when my all of earthly good - my world of felicity - was comprised in such a little space, within the walls of that old-fashioned parlour, here the firelight flashed broad and bright on the warm damask curtains and I sat on that low footstool by the hearth at the feet of one who never tired of telling those rich old tales and legends of other days . . . Her portraits lived and breathed - uncles, aunts, cousins, a bewigged and brocaded host made to re-act their former parts on the great stage." Her grandmother too was a great teller of tales, so Caroline's narrative gifts must have come from her mother's family. She was certainly brought up to be aware of their former station in society - note the bewigged and brocaded ancestors in the stories. Mother and grandmother made it plain that they came from no peasant stock.

Drawing lessons with her mother were a special delight. She would lay the sketch of a purple stock upon her lap -

> Then hang upon her shoulder, shrinking back
> With a child's bashfulness, all hope and fear
> Shunning and courting notice ... Mother's love
> Thought it perfection.

Anne Bowles shines from her daughter's pages as a warm, high spirited and cultured woman, capably presiding over her elderly household, for there was Great Grandmother, Anne Durrell too, and their Norman-French nurse, also from Jersey, known to Caroline always as *Ma Bonne*. Her great grandmother died when Caroline was only three, but her grandmother was a devoted companion.

> And one - the good, the gentle, the beloved,
> My Mother's mother. Still methinks I see
> Her gracious countenance. The unruffled brow
> The soft blue eye, the still carnationed cheek
> Unwrinkled yet.
> Even now that placid smile I see
> That kindly beamed on all, but chief on me!

A friend of the family has left a portrait of Grandmother, lightly spiced with malice which offsets Caroline's, painted with a more loving eye.

"Madame Burrard as she grew old, used to be carried from the porch at Buckland Cottage to her pew in church. There she bowed and curtsied to her friends before the service began ... She stood up in her little high-heeled shoes of black velvet with silver buckles, and a diamond crescent sparkled just in front of her powdered hair which was drawn up on a cushion under a lace cap and hood. The rest of her dress was invariably black, though she also wore the lace ruffles, neckerchief and apron that had been in fashion when she was a child." In fact Madame was wearing head-dress and clothes after the traditions of her beloved Jersey.

The death of her great grandmother was Caroline's first experience of grief, the first break in the magic circle round her. Long after she could remember her violent tears, but she was honest enough to confess being diverted from them by the sight of herself in the mirror dressed for the first time in black with a very long crêpe sash!

When all her relations were busy, there still remained *Ma Bonne* to look after Caroline and tell her stories of Longueville, the great house in Jersey, from which she had come with Madeleine Burrard. For example, here is the child's great uncle, his portly form -

> ... magnificent in rich brocade
> And broidered rosebuds, and rough woven gold,
> Half down his thigh the long-flapped waistcoat fell,

while the ladies were resplendent in silks and damasks worn over whaleboned stiffened petticoats which could stand up alone - all these figures moving in stately paces about the chateau and past the dovecote of a thousand doves. Others paced the triple avenue of great trees leading to the common world. So even as a child, Caroline lived an unusual amount in the past. Nurse never laid by her origins, always wore the high Jersey cap, large ear-rings and short jacket, never ceased to speak with a French accent.

When Caroline was five, Lymington was threatened by a serious outbreak of smallpox. The churchwardens called upon everyone to have the inoculation, but this had not yet been perfected: out of some twelve hundred who were treated, at least twenty died of the inoculation itself. One can only imagine the dread at Buckland Cottage, then the horror when Caroline, everyone's darling, was smitten with smallpox and soon so ill that she was given up for lost. But *Ma Bonne* would not be beaten, never shrank away, nursing her devotedly through long feverish nights and days, so that she did slowly begin to recover, only to see her nurse sicken with the same serious and highly contagious disease. Caroline not only grew better, she was left with hardly any of those disfiguring scars which were such a hideous legacy of smallpox. *Ma Bonne* also recovered, left with only a few marks -

> Let me rest my cheek even now
> On thy dear shoulder, printed with a mark
> Indelible of suffering borne for me.

This is the first of Caroline's illnesses of which we hear: she was always a delicate child and would spend her whole life battling with ill health.

Once better though, she returned to all the enjoyments of Buckland. The cottage stood (and still stands) among fields and trees half a mile from the town of Lymington, built at right angles to the main Southampton road on the corner of Hollywood Lane, its only neighbours a farm and a manor house on the other side of the lane which led down to an open space known as the Waste of Buckland, where outdoor revels such as maypole dancing were held. Nearly opposite rose the green ramparts of Buckland Rings, the remains of an Iron Age Fort. The cottage itself, of mellow brick and russet tiles, built earlier in the century was modest in size for so large a household, but made up for this, in Caroline's eyes at least, with its vast, rambling garden, secluded from the road. Undulating lawns dipped into thickets of rhododendron, narrow paths wound away between shrubberies of lilac and bay to secret forgotten corners shadowed by elms and limes, while stone steps curved down to a hidden level, showered in its season with petals of cherry and broom. Nightingales came to nest every spring.

Caroline had her own patch of garden, full of wild flowers lovingly transplanted from the country round, primroses, bluebells, aconites and violets. With seeds she was impatient, often digging them up after three days to see if they were growing, and if so, planting them again a little nearer to the top. Close by, her swing hung in a willow tree and all around the garden lived her pets and pensioners and patients. Princess Hemjunah, the toad, a one-legged bullfinch, a lame hare, a wounded squirrel - of course they changed over the years - while just over the hedge in the paddock in which he had been born, lived her own small pony Juba, 'fleet as the whirlwind.'

This kingdom was ruled by white-haired old Ephraim, the gardener, who was plainly as fond of her as everybody else, since he carved her a wheelbarrow and a set of garden tools exactly right for her size, brought her the first ripe strawberries every summer and taught her the names of his plants. He must have had to grit his teeth very hard at times though; once the pet hare ate all his best lettuce AND the early peas, while mouse traps, freshly baited with toasted cheese each night, failed to catch a single mouse. Willy the lamb was not much trouble at first, a pretty sight, pattering after Caroline indoors and out, but time went by, and Willy drew near to ram's estate, growing formidable horns. Soon he had chased Chloé, the spaniel, butted the butcher's boy and hooked down the washing from the lines. Then came the final act.

> It was the time of blossoms, and my father
> Who in trim gardens much delight did take
> Was scanning with a gardener's prideful eye
> His neat espaliers
> Thick set with bloom - deep blushing like the morn,

when suddenly the petals of a nearby tree began to shower down, whitening the path. Another butting charge destroyed all fruiting chances of the golden pippin. Ephraim and the maids were summoned, Willy captured and led away, a bunch of apple blossom still dangling from his jaws, and this time not all Caroline's blandishments could save his being banished to the farm.

The garden was an immensely important part of Caroline's world, where she could escape the pressures of people, however loving: without it she might well have grown up a prissy, spoiled miss. Here she could grovel in the earth of her own patch, climb trees, romp with the dogs, scramble through hedges for a glimpse of rabbits and became a proper tomboy - the despair of Jane, the maid, who was supposed to keep her neat and pretty, but was daily confronted by frocks and petticoats all torn and muddy.

Though surrounded by adults who were particularly good storytellers, learning to read for herself opened up a whole new world. She devoured *The Arabian Nights, Gulliver's Travels, Pilgrim's Progress* and of course, in that household The Bible. Later she discovered poetry, Marlowe, Herbert, Thompson's *Seasons* and Pope. Ballads were already familiar from her mother's singing. But too much poetry had a strange, intoxicating effect. After reading a poem she would feel impelled to write one herself with the same rhythm and rhyme pattern and could settle to nothing else till it was done to her satisfaction. When Caroline refused to sleep at night till she had finished composing her latest effort, her mother grew worried over this precocious daughter and took to hiding the poetry books.

As she grew older, the garden became not only her great escape from being a good little girl, but the private place where she could play out the dreams and fantasies fed by so much reading. An example of this was Gesner's *Death of Abel*, a book famous in its time, which led her to set up an altar.

> And in a certain unfrequented nook
> Of our long rambling garden, fenced about
> By thorns and bushes, thick with summer leaves
> And threaded by a little water course - uprose full soon
> A mound of mossy turf.

This she daily decorated with flowers.

Solitary and dreamy, rocking to and fro on the swing in the willow tree, she would conjure castles and spirits, all the wild characters from the *Arabian Nights*, and later, people from novels such as *Pamela* and *Grandison*, with whom to have adventures and conversations.

Outside, children her age and younger worked long hours, bird scaring, stone picking, weeding, or gathering rushes to make a few extra pennies to eke out the family income, which might be twenty pounds a year if several of its members were working. Farm labourers' children could seldom be spared to go to school, besides, that could cost threepence a week. They lived on bread, milkless tea, bacon and whatever vegetables they could grow. In 1795, when Caroline was nine, the price of a loaf more than doubled, which led to rioting. When Sarah Rogers, in nearby Fordingbridge, seized some butter to sell at a fair price, she was sentenced to three month's hard labour by Winchester Assizes. As war with France forced up the price of food, few labourers' families could manage without parish relief.

The poor were growing poorer still, even while Caroline rocked to and fro on her swing.

The rich were doing splendidly. In 1785, Lord Dorchester, in the adjoining county, took a dislike to the hamlet of Milton Abbess, which he could see from his windows - so he had it moved further off. George III was a frequent visitor to Lymington, parading the town to the cheers of the populace and usually staying at Walhampton, the Burrard mansion. Caroline never mentions this grand house as any part of her childhood: the excursion she remembers with the greatest enthusiasm is the walk across the river to the neighbouring village of Boldre to visit its parson.

William Gilpin, for twenty five years headmaster of Cheam School was given the living of Boldre as a country retreat when he retired. But he found, "the lower class of parishioner little better than a gang of gypsies, neglected and exposed to every temptation of pillage and robbery." So, being a man of immense energies and kindness, he set about altering the place, building a poor house and a school, meanwhile writing and illustrating the large volumes of *Forest Scenery*, for which he is still remembered, and drawing pictures of the surrounding countryside to be sold to provide an endowment for the school.

Caroline and Jane would set off about four o'clock in order to arrive for six o'clock tea. They walked down Hollywood Lane and along the river bank to a wooden footbridge (the scene of a gruesome tragedy in one of Caroline's adult poems) overhung with willow and alder, the shady banks bright with kingcups, meadowsweet and purple loosestrife in their season, with moorhens skittering for cover in the reeds and beady-eyed mallard gliding past. But then they must leave this cool green world behind and begin the long open climb towards the Rectory.

Boldre is still a scattered village, its houses often far apart and secluded behind high walls or hedges along the lanes rambling down to the river, winding through lush meadows and open park land. The Rectory is a fine Georgian house at the top of the hill.

Here Caroline was lovingly welcomed, divested of her hat, tippet and gloves, her brow cooled with elder flower water, then bade to rest till tea time, but though tired from the walk, she fidgetted restlessly about till she was at last allowed her heart's desire, to knock on the study door and say, as she had done countless times before, "It's me."

> How holy was the calm of that small room!
> How tenderly the evening light stole in,
> Here and there touching with a golden gleam
> Bookshelf or picture frame.

Here for a moment she was struck dumb with loving awe, but the old man, however busy, soon laid aside his pen and spread out his latest drawings for her, encouraging her to comment and even criticise his work. Long after, Caroline would look back and say this was how she learned to draw, and she was to become an accomplished artist.

William Gilpin's influence can still be seen in Boldre, the small stone church on its wooded knoll, which he had restored is still constantly refurbished by local craftsmen. A house called Gilpin's Cottage stands at the corner of School Lane. Opposite, Gilpin built a poorhouse. When this was pulled down and the new school built in its place, his memorial tablet was transferred to it.

He lies buried in the churchyard beneath a table tomb, curiously inscribed, 'In a quiet mansion beneath this stone, secure from the afflictions and still more dangerous enjoyments of life, lie the remains of William Gilpin.'

Boldre Church was to see the crucial day of Caroline's life, but for the moment it was back with the maid to the shelter of home.

Little of the outside world disturbed Caroline's girlhood. The revolution in France with its slaughter of the nobility had forced many officers to flee for their lives to England, where they were collected into regiments to fight in Flanders. One of these, The Loyal Emigrants, was stationed in Lymington town, while another, The Royal French Marine was actually quartered in The Old Manor House, just across the lane from Buckland Cottage, others occupying the nearby farm. But Caroline dreams on, reading Tasso and Alexander Pope, probably books already to be found about the house. By the beginning of the new century, Caroline was in her teens and had been reading 'grown up' books for years, but just as the French Revolution seemed far away, the great impact of the Romantic revolution in literature had not breached the walls either.

William Cowper who died in 1800, would have seemed an ideal choice, with his gentle passion for jackdaws, spaniels and hares, his piety and narrow horizons, but he is not mentioned. She had not read any of Burns' rumbustious tales such as *Tam O'Shanter*, or Chatterton's mock-medieval lyrics or Blake's wild visions. (A certain Robert Southey, then in his late twenties, had recently published a long narrative poem called *Joan of Arc*) It was the publication of *Lyrical Ballads* by Coleridge and Wordsworth which altered English poetry for ever - there had never been anything like the simple language and clarity of *The Ancient Mariner* except the old traditional ballads. Some applauded, many were scandalised. Caroline would read them later in life, but a writer's style is formed when she is young and impressionable. She continued to read conservative and wordy works of the previous century, often second-rate writers such as Gesner, Harvey and Taylor now quite forgotten. This is important in the development of her own poetry, which has been likened to Crabbe and Cowper though never to her own contemporaries. Caroline just went on writing in her own way which was old-fashioned, even in its own time. In spite of her loving family, she was often alone and books became, if anything, over-important -

> I was an only child, and never knew
> The social pleasures of a schoolgirl's life.
> Books were my playfellows.

This was written many years later and does sound a little wistful. There were few visitors. Uncle Philip, her mother's brother, came one day to supervise the pruning of a cistus among the roots of which lived Caroline's pet toad. Carried away, he practically felled the poor tree and 'The Princess' was never seen again. Sometimes Caroline would go visiting on her beloved pony, Juba. If she did go to see Uncle Harry Burrard at Calshot Castle, or the other Uncle Harry, her mother's cousin, in the grand house at Walhampton across the river, these were not important enough memories to be celebrated in *The Birthday*.

Instead there is a lovingly detailed description of afternoons with Prissy. Anne Bowles claimed relationship with Lord Herbert of Cherbury and kept green memories of ancestral chateaux in Jersey, so it seems highly unlikely that she ever knew how many hours her daughter spent in the gardener's cottage, where Ephraim's wife practised a magic quite different from the Reverend Gilpin's. In an earlier century she would probably have been called a witch. Before her marriage, Priscilla had worked as companion to A Lady, and still walked out in her employer's cut-down clothes, a black satin cloak, for example, only a thought embrowned with age. She also spoke 'refined', and rejoiced in a cottage stuffed with treasures which included books on warts, moles and the virtues of herbs.

> Deep read was she in varied lore profound -
> Divinity, Romance and Pharmacy,
> And - so the neighbours whispered - in deep things
> Passing the parson's wisdom.

It was Jane, the maid deputed to look after Caroline, who took her to the cottage for she was a close friend of Prissy's. The visit would fall into two sessions, both of which Caroline loved. First of all there would be piping hot buttered oven cake and tea with cream and sugar, then a time on her own when Jane and Prissy put their heads together and spoke in whispered tones of 'women's things'. Now she could browse on horrors in Fox's *Book of the Martyrs*, find the cat who always had one kitten the same size, the one-eyed cockatoo with gouty legs, a stuffed pug-dog, and best of all the entrancing cuckoo clock. Prissy's cottage is important in Caroline's life for here she first day-dreamed of the future.

Every girl of her age and station was brought up to envisage a handsome husband and a fine establishment, but while the women murmured together of the latest pregnancy or ways of terminating one, Caroline dreamed of independence.

> When I'm a woman I'll have, quoth I,
> Not settlements and pin-money and spouse
> Appendant, but in unencumbered right
> Of womanhood - a house and cuckoo clock!

This wish was to come true: Prissy left her the cuckoo clock when she died, and Caroline won her independence, but like many wishes fulfilled neither brought her great happiness.

When she was fifteen, her much loved father suffered an apoplectic seizure, dying soon afterwards, and her childhood ended. After a suitable period of mourning, Caroline and her mother came out from behind the sheltering walls of Buckland Cottage and found a very different world awaiting them.

chapter two

A whirl of dissipation

The leafy road outside led down into Lymington, a small sea port, set between vast stretches of coastal mudflats and the wilds of the New Forest, its harbour, the river mouth, lying opposite the green, western shores of the Isle of Wight. A wide main street sloped down to narrow cobbled passages leading to the quays along the west bank and also the salt pans - a rough quarter where the Press Gang roamed, gulls screamed over discarded fish guts and there were drunken brawls most nights, outside the brothel.

The High Street was lined with elegant houses, Tudor, Queen Anne or the modern Georgian with its fine front doors and large windows, homes of prosperous merchants. There were Assembly Rooms and hotels such as The Angel, catering for the coach trade and at the top, the ivy clad stones of St. Thomas's church. But beneath all this respectability lay tunnels leading to the river bank, one from The Angel itself, for smuggling continued to thrive through all the confusions of war. So Caroline's Lymington was a town of extraordinary contrasts.

And the war came closer. Napoleon stared across the English Channel. The local militia paraded in their white uniforms, armed with pikes. In 1803 when Caroline was seventeen, the threat of invasion was taken so seriously that plans were made to evacuate the town: every wagon to be found in the farms round about was registered and numbered, including the one in the farm next door to Buckland Cottage, so that they could be called out at a moment's notice.

In spite of the war, and even in part because of it, Lymington was still a fashionable resort. French aristocrats, fleeing from the terror of the revolution and the fall of the guillotine to southern England made it their centre. Also a large body of French Royalists, with officers from Germany and Italy were quartered there. Above all, the King himself, popular 'Farmer George,' the first of the Hanoverians to behave like an English gentleman, often paid visits, usually connected with his friend Sir Harry Burrard Neale. The Burrard family had bought the Walhampton estate above the east bank of the Lymington River in 1668, thus acquiring also a seat in parliament - Burrards represented Lymington until 1832.

When Sir Harry Burrard married Grace Neale, he added her family name to his own. By now an admiral in charge of the Mediterranean Fleet, he was also a close friend of the royal family. In 1804, for example, George III, Queen Charlotte and the Princesses with attendant court, came to stay at Walhampton. The King held a reception at the Town Hall and afterwards paraded the High Street, "A tall stout gentleman in cocked hat, top boots and buckskins, wearing a gold-buttoned bright green coat." Sir Harry always invited many local friends to visit to demonstrate their loyalty in this time of stress: Caroline and her mother would have been family guests. So Bath might have its spa for fashionable taking of the waters, but Lymington had its royal connection and just as later, there was a ball on the eve of Waterloo, so the social whirl was at its height as the French armies massed to invade England.

Caroline loved dancing. The other Sir Harry, her uncle at Calshot Castle, gave her all the tickets she needed for military balls. A friend described her at this time as having, "dark grey eyes, a finely formed forehead, a slight graceful figure, a hand deft and light with the needle, pen and pencil, with a shower of golden curls falling round her face." Others wrote of them as auburn. Long after, in a poem called *Once upon a Time*, she describes herself when young.

... yes, these locks of mine
Clustered once with golden shine
Temples, neck and shoulders round
Richly gushing if unbound
Well nigh downward to the knee.

Her mother accompanied her to the balls to chaperone, as was proper. Surely French nobles and English aristocrats vied to dance with Caroline, court her lively, petite person? Of course financially she would hardly seem to be 'a good catch.' Uncharted by letters or notebooks, her late teens and early twenties remain the most mysterious part of her life.

One evening at Buckland, while getting ready for a dance, Caroline decided not to go after all, but her mother went, just the same. After years of seclusion looking after her elderly household, Anne Bowles was obviously enjoying her new social life. When she returned from Lymington Town Hall, she found that Caroline had spent the evening making a large and finely detailed drawing called *Packing up after the Ball*, exactly as she had just seen it. This was later printed by Charles Josef Hullmandel, a pioneer of lithography.

Packing up certainly reveals that Caroline was a talented artist, no mere sketcher of pretty views like so many women of her time, but more important than that, it shows she had a wicked eye! For the whole picture is a satire, gentler than Cruikshank's but certainly edged with malice. Two soldiers sitting down, very slim and foppish, are whispering behind their hands evidently appraising the females, a group of young ladies in long flounced dresses collect cloaks from a table and the chaperones are settling grotesquely tall bonnets over their high-piled hair - one is plump and ugly, another has a large nose. All these gathered in a horseshoe shape and in its very centre stands a real figure of fun, a short fat woman with a moon face and balloon-like bosoms, struggling to keep her balance on a pair of pattens, the wooden oversoles everyone is strapping on to protect their shoes from the mud outside. All the older ladies wear a homely, countrified air, as if not really happy in all their finery.

The scene is precisely set in the old town hall with its panelled walls and long staircase, where further groups are descending in the background, while a half open door reveals a crowd of servants waiting on the step with umbrellas and lanterns ready to escort their mistresses home, the smallest boy wearing the tallest hat as if to make up for his size. The technical skills Caroline may well have learned from the artist of *Forest Scenery*, but *Packing up after the Ball* also shows her photographic eye for detail and a naughty sense of humour which is hardly ever allowed to surface in her poems.

Even if her financial prospects were not that good, it would have been surprising if such a pretty, gifted and witty girl met no admirers. The only information about this time is provided by a friend who many years later wrote a long obituary article, signed E.O. containing these enigmatic sentences. "Caroline did indeed return the long attachment of one in every respect worthy of her, but it was at last decided by a family conclave that her engagement should be broken off owing to want of sufficient means on the gentleman's part. She submitted."

This crisis in Caroline's life is still shrouded in mystery. Is it true? She does not sound like a young woman who would submit so easily if she were truly in love. No journals or letters survive from this time. Nothing in her poems gives any clue as to who the fiancé might be or to her state of mind at this time. Though she was to spend a great deal of writing time looking back upon the past, it is never to a time of lost love in the romantic sense. She had always been and would continue to be, extremely close to her mother which makes it seem unlikely that Anne Bowles would have forbidden a match which promised her beloved daughter happiness, even if the suitor did not quite live up to her traditions of chateaux in Jersey.

One can only speculate on the clues provided. The Bowles themselves lived in a modest enough way, so the gentleman must indeed have lacked means if he could not provide Caroline with a similar establishment to Buckland Cottage. If it was a long attachment, was it a relative? Cousins often married in the nineteenth century. Sir Harry had four younger sons and there were also Bowles cousins of suitable age. Perhaps someone who lived close by, since Buckland and the neighbouring village of Boldre had various prosperous houses half hidden behind high walls or bowered in trees - many of them still there.

If E.O.'s account is true, it is odd that Caroline was later to repudiate the companions of her youth and even breathe a criticism of her mother's judgement. Looking back on these years in 1828, she was to write, "It is sad to tell that all the best years of my life were (from strange circumstances) passed among those who had little fear of God and it was God's special mercy that I never lost sight of that, though compelled to associate with those unprincipled people, too many of them talented and clever and most agreeable and by that means utterly duping my dear Mother. A strange whirl of dissipation and danger of all sorts I lived in, too often drawn for a time into the vortex, but always, thank God, with a sense of danger - a something within me that was not of the world I lived in . . . So I have been an arch deceiver. Among one set of people - the light, the wild, the unprincipled votaries of pleasure, I was comparatively cold, proud and reserved, and older than my elders and thought a pattern of prudence: and when with those whose opinion I really valued, I was the gayest and giddiest of the gay and giddy, the promoter of all mischief and the deepest in all scapes."

She adds archly, "My autobiography would not be unentertaining, but I will take special care not to favour the public with it."

Two years later she wrote in like vein. "I would not live my youth again for all the world, but some of the illusions I would give worlds to renew . . . it took too many years (from the age of scarce fifteeen to twenty six) to depress and at last almost crush the elasticity of my spirit and the looking back upon all the strange troubles I then had to steer through effects my mind far more painfully now, than at the time of their actual existence. All through that interval I knew that for the most part, precious time was slipping past me, unimproved, wasted, worse than wasted and yet I could not help myself. Is it not sad to look back on such a youth and think how late I began to live?"

Her poems were equally enigmatic. *That's What We Are*, for example describes this period when she was apparently torn in two.

> Despairingly I sought the social scene
> Sound - motion - action - interchange of words,
> Scarcely of mind - rare privilege.
>   ... We talked
> Oh how we talked - discussed and solved all questions -
> Religion, morals, manners, politics,
> Physics and metaphysics, books and authors,
> Fashion and dress, our neighbours and ourselves.

What made these years so sinister in her memory? Does she mean *moral* danger, when she uses that word?

One of the best poems in her lighter style, *To the Sweet Scented Cyclamen*, charmingly describes, at the beginning, the interior of Buckland Cottage, Mother pouring tea while Caroline's friends wandered about the garden or sang or played the flute - 'Young, happy hearts.' But in the later verses she describes the years when 'all are gone.'

Some far away in other lands -
In this, some worse than dead -
Some in their graves lie quietly -
One slumbering in the deep, deep sea -
All gone! All lost! All fled.

What was this fate worse than death?

It is much easier to paint a true picture when Caroline escapes from the social whirl to Uncle Harry Burrard and his wife Hannah, who were both specially fond of her. (Of their five sons, they were to lose two, Paul and John in 1809, and another, William, in 1813, in the wars) Looking back on these years, Caroline was to write, "It is impossible to express my happiness during about three months of the years, when with my dear Uncle at Calshot or in London. I recollect feeling, when I first got close to him as if I might throw off all guard over myself and be as young as my years and as confiding and as thoughtless as my nature. It was like stepping from a creaking plank across a chasm on to hard, firm ground. So I have played two very different characters."

Calshot Castle is a rather grand name for a fort, shaped like a gigantic cotton reel, built by Henry VIII on the end of a spit of land guarding the entrance to Southampton Water. In 1774 the gatehouse was largely rebuilt to provide living quarters for the Governor of the castle, an office usually bestowed as a reward for service to the Country. Sir Harry Burrard, who had fought in many campaigns, was given the Governorship of Calshot in 1787. By this time he was a lieutenant general.

On a fine day, the castle is an exhilarating place, with Southampton Water and the Solent lapping about it on three sides and only a narrow strip of land joining it to the New Forest: from its castellated battlements Caroline could see the north coast of the Isle of Wight, east and west along the Solent, up the Water to Southampton and even to the chalk hills beyond Portsmouth, while out on the sheltered sea all round moved ships of every kind, tall-sailed frigates carrying thirty six guns, merchant ships, fast cutters, fishing boats, dinghies and the great Navy ships heading for Portsmouth Harbour further east.

The round fort is surrounded by a courtyard, in itself contained by the great outer wall, and here between the buttresses they managed to grow flowers and creepers. Sir Harry was once very angry with a visitor who suggested putting up artificial palm trees, strenghthened with iron! A salt sou'wester blows here for the greater part of the year, but contemporary sketches certainly show the ramparts softened by flourishing greenery: according to Caroline there was myrtle, jessamine, roses and heliotrope, all named in a poem set at Calshot, *The Night Scented Stock*.

Here she is asking a friend to return at night to enjoy the flower's fragrance -

> ... when the Lady Moon
> Looks down on that bastioned wall,
> When the twinkling stars dance silently
> On the rippling surface of the sea
> And the heavy night dews fall.

All the Burrard boys were grown up by now, and away from home. Even so, the living quarters in the gatehouse must have been rather cramped. On the landward side it is stone faced with arrow slits, a drawbridge across the moat leading to the entrance tunnel beneath some of the living rooms, but the rear, inside the courtyard is revealed as Georgian red brick. Narrow stairs led up to the three main rooms which were originally panelled. E.O. wrote, "There were many delightful houses among the walks of the New Forest where Caroline stayed at Calshot Castle, her uncle being the governor and after his death (1813) still home of his widow. Deep embrasures of windows formed a recess for reading and writing, the walls covered with books, carvings and pictures by various members of the family. The heavy buttresses were made to afford shelter to flowers and abundance of climbing plants. The woods that surround Luttrell's Folly were not far off. The old fortress was as much home to Caroline as Buckland."

Only the fort itself had stone walls thick enough to provide deep embrasures - did the Burrards occupy one of its three floors, as well as the gatehouse?

Here at last Caroline could find something of the peaceful loving atmosphere which had enveloped her before the death of her father, in fact this was what she went on craving for many years, to be the youngest in a family circle, apparently neither seeking a mate like most of her contemporaries, nor setting up an independant life, as Prissy's cuckoo clock had once made her dream of doing.

Uncle Harry himself needed all the family support possible, never mind he was a distinguished general who had fought in North Africa and Flanders. In 1808, during the Peninsular War, he was sent out to Portugal to succeed Sir Arthur Wellesley, who had just beaten off the French army at the battle of Vimeiro. Under the impression that the French were about to bring up large reinforcements, Sir Arthur, Sir Hew Dalrymple and General Harry Burrard concluded the Convention of Cintra, by which any advance was forbidden and the defeated French allowed to go home, taking their equipment with them This caving-in caused a great public outcry: all three men were recalled to London for an inquiry, and though exonerated from blame, much criticism lingered in the air.

So it must have been an enormous relief for Sir Harry to return to his almost-island castle, the warmth of his family and the staunch affection of his niece. He and Caroline often went on long walks together. Even years later, she would rush to her Uncle's defence at the very mention of the Convention of Cintra.

But it was a sad time at the castle too, for the following year, Sir Harry's second son, Paul, an aide-de-camp to Sir John Moore, was killed, like his general, at the battle of Corunna, and John, his fourth son, died also.

Since the giddy social whirl of Lymington took up so much of her time at Buckland, Caroline's writing, which had continued ever since she was a small child, flourished best at Calshot, where she could wander the shore and the castle walls or ride off into the woods. Though obviously a high spirited young woman with a naughty wit, her poetry tended always toward tragic subjects, indeed later she would say she could only write poetry when deeply moved and for her this seemed to mean tragedy rather than joy.

During these years she had begun to draught a long narrative poem in the metrical style of Walter Scott, then very popular, but with none of his lively action. Ellen Fitzarthur lives at the rectory with her widowed father. When a half drowned young sailor is rescued and brought there, she nurses him back to health and falls in love. When he leaves, she goes with him, but soon he deserts her and her bastard child. Homeless, she sets out for the rectory, only to find it cold and dark. Searching the graveyard for her mother's grave, she finds her father's name added to the tombstone.

Caroline was still writing to please herself, with no thought of publication, so the lugubrious subject was not chosen to suit any editor or potential readers. To the late twentieth century mind it seems both dreary and hackneyed, but the nineteenth century encouraged just such writing. Wordsworth wrote on similar themes in poems such as *The Thorn* or *Ruth*, in which the deserted heroine goes mad. Later in the century the story might well have inspired Thomas Hardy. Any anthology of the period will yield half a dozen poems written *To a Dying Infant*, so the story of Ellen Fitzarthur must be seen in the context of its time.

In 1813 Caroline lost the second father-figure in her life: Uncle Harry died, to her deep grief. Two years later, the long war was over and Caroline with her mother was at last able to make the long planned visit to the home of their ancestors, Jersey.

Caroline's descent from the great house of Longueville, east of St Helier, was the consequence of eavesdropping. In 1750 George Burrard of Lymington visited Jersey and met a Mademoiselle D, who was handsome and rich (also rather haughty and remote). His family ignored her character and were delighted to arrange a marriage as soon as his regiment returned from Flanders. Meanwhile George and Mademoiselle D were to keep in touch by writing frequent letters.

"Great was the young soldier's happiness when, as time passed, each letter from his sweetheart became more delightful than the last. She had appeared to him rather cold and imperious and he fancied she had accepted his addresses too much as a matter of course, but her letters undeceived him and left him in no doubt of her affection. They contained the fullest accounts of her daily life at the chateau, with all the little adventures that befell herself and her friends, described in the most amusing way and with a childlike zest and womanly grace that promised delightful companionship in the future."

So as soon as a short leave came up, George hurried back to Jersey and the grand house, only to be told that no one was at home - the Seigneur and his wife were away and Mademoiselle D and her cousin, Madeleine Durrell were in the summer-house at the end of the nut avenue. So he lost no time in looking for them.

"Full of hope and joy he stood for a moment on that glowing afternoon near the pretty pavilion, afraid of startling his promised bride by so sudden an appearance. The summer leaves were thick and the noisette roses clustered thickly around it, but he heard a well-known voice exclaim, "Will you never have done, Madeleine, with that tiresome letter? It is lucky we write so alike. I should hardly have patience to copy all you find to say."

Of course George broke off his engagement and eventually married la petite Madeleine, the writer of all those delightful letters, and many years later, teller of tales to her granddaughetr, Caroline.

George lost nothing through his change of fiancée, for Madeleine was the daughter of Jean Durrell, Attorney General and Seigneur of the Manor of Longueville. Caroline had never tired of stories of the great house, of how her stately great grandmother sat enthroned among her sewing maids, of the ancient gateway proudly bearing the family coat of arms leading to a triple avenue of noble trees and the immense round dovecote with its thousand perches - this was doubly significant for only those with seignorial rights were allowed to build dovecotes. Some of the stories came from *Ma Bonne* who remembered Longueville as possibly grander than it really was, since she had been taken in to it as a young maid. But the main door of the house was so wide, the locals said you could drive a farm cart through it!

Eighteenth century drawings show an enclosed courtyard entered by an imposing stone archway and there are records of a manorial chapel. Madeleine herself inherited Longueville after the deaths of her brothers, but on her death the house seems to have reverted to the Jersey Burrards who let the house fall derelict. The Rev. Bateman who carried out extensive repairs in the 1860's mentions the chapel being pulled down some fifty years before.

So by the time Caroline came to Longueville, there was a sad decline - better not to have braved the rough sea voyage but let it remain a castle in her mind. Years later she was to write -

> I've seen the ancient gateway where it stands
> An isolated arch. The noble trees
> (A triple avenue) its proud approach
> Gone as they n'er had been: the dovecote tower
> A desecrated ruin; the old house -
> Dear Nurse! full fain am I to weep with thee
> The faded glories of 'the good old time.'

The old family home is now an hotel.

Back at Buckland, life resumed its even tenor. All that wild social life had dropped away when Caroline was twenty six, according to one of her letters, though she does not say what happened in 1813 to bring this about. A year passes in writing and sketching, paying calls with her mother, writing long letters, visiting Calshot and working in her beloved garden among its lofty trees and winding paths. Around Buckland she rode her pony and exercised her dogs.

The busy turnpike road to Southampton passed right by the cottage, its toll house lying a few yards down the hill beside what was then called The Crown Inn, but turning off this were leafy lanes such as Silver Street leading round Buckland Rings, the green acres of an Iron Age fort, and others running down to the willows and alders of the river bank or over Boldre Bridge to Boldre village. Beyond stretched the vast heaths and woodlands of the New Forest.

A few neighbouring houses stood half-hidden behind tall oaks and elms, among them Buckland Manor Farm at the end of its long avenue, Little Buckland Farm, now the Old Manor House, and the inn. Buckland Cottage itself had originally been a small dwelling, called Soper's Tenement, while the land around it, leased by the Bowles family, was called Chantry Mead, since it was the site of a chapel or chantry built in the thirteeth century by Roger de Bocland. (The cottage was called Chantry Mead for a period this century) At the foot of the hill stood the first milestone out of Lymington, to which Caroline remembered taking her very first walk outside the garden.

> Here, the goal attained
> They set me up on the old stone to rest
> And called me Woman! Baby now no more.

Altogether, Buckland was a delightful spot in which to live and full of history, from the pre-historic to the personal: in the larger world it was a time of great change.

The King, once so popular as Farmer George, no longer visited Lymington: old and sick, he was shut away, while his son, the Prince Regent with his profligate tastes, his gambling and his mistresses was fast losing all the goodwill so readily extended to his father. Shouting mobs took the place of cheering crowds: once a stone broke the window of the royal carriage.

The government feared revolution, as well they might: a recession had led to dire poverty and parliament itself rested on rotten foundations. Old Sarum, an uninhabited earthwork just north of Salisbury, sent a member to Parliament, but a big, fast growing town such as Birmingham had no representative at all.

With no one to listen to them, people began to riot, in Scotland against the Clearances where tenants were everywhere evicted for the sake of sheep, in Dorset against enclosure of commonland and in Hampshire against threshing machines that threatened employment.

Country people were left dreadfully poor after the steep rise in bread prices. In Salisbury, cottagers could only afford one fire a week so had to take it in turns to cook, with seven pots to each fire. Many flocked to the new industrial towns to find work in factories where even their children could be employed and seven year olds worked thirteen or fourteen hours a day in conditions so cruel that Caroline, several years later, was moved to write a book about them.

One of the most galling sights for a poor man with wife and children to feed, must have been a prosperous parkland, kept well stocked for the gentry with partridge and pheasant, deer and hare. A Hampshire man was transported for seven years for owning a rabbit net. At least the Commoners of the New Forest did not lose their rights to pasture beasts or take turf and firewood.

One night in January 1817 Caroline and her mother spent a cosy evening by their own log fire, the lamplight gleaming on portraits of ancestors and tall eastern vases brought back from India: they sewed, wrote letters, read to each other, talked peacefully together till the end of the evening. Caroline tells what happened next, after she had remembered a visit they were to pay soon.

"'Oh Mother, how I wish this day a fortnight would come.'

'Do not think that,' Mother replied in a tone that startled and made me look round at her as I was leaving the room, and yet in my obstinate impatience I repeated,

'But I must wish it, Mother dear, and I will wish it.'

'You have wished away your time,' she said 'and in a fortnight hence how you may repent your impatience - you may have no Mother then.'

She looked as I had never seen her look before, and spoke as I had never heard her speak; but she was in excellent health, and afterwards, when she saw how I was struck and affected, laughed at my superstition and said she did not know why she had spoken thus - 'It was without thought or meaning,' and she seemed to forget it."

But a few days later, at the age of sixty three, Anne Bowles suffered a sudden, massive stroke and before that fortnight was out, was buried among the Burrard graves in Lymington churchyard.

The shock to Caroline was all the more harsh because her mother had seemed in good health: living together for sixteen years since the death of Charles, they had become very close - dear friends as well as mother and daughter. *Ma Bonne*, herself growing old and frail, was now the only one left of that loving circle which had sheltered Caroline from the world. A deeply religious woman, Caroline longed in her grief to join her family in heaven and was moved to write this sonnet -

Dark rolling clouds in wild confusion driven,
Obscure the full-orbed moon. In all the heaven
One only star - the appointed evening light -
Beams mildly forth: like friendly Pharos bright
That, kindled on some summit, streams
Wide o'er the ocean paths. Its far-off beams
First seen by him who on the silent deck
Paces his lonely watch - a glimmering speck,
Doubtful in distance. But his homeward eye
Is keen the faithful beacon to descry,
And mine, like his, impatient to explore -
With friends and kindred thronged - the distant shore,
Is fixed on that lone star, whose lovely ray
Points to a happier home, the heavenward way.

As it always does, death brought business affairs to bring her down to earth. The lease of Buckland Cottage was left to her, but the capital sum was put in charge of a trustee - and this vanished. She wrote, "My pecuniary distress is the result of my guardian's fraudulent bankruptcy, from which only a little pittance was saved from the wreck." This was not enough to maintain Buckland Cottage, so she was left, not only without adequate income, but with the necessity to move from the only home she had ever known, furnished with a thousand memories of the loved ones she had lost. This woman who could only write when deeply moved, now poured out her anguish in poetry.

One poem, *On the Near Prospect of Leaving Home 1818*, has a particularly revealing verse. Friends have been trying to cheer her up, saying there are other places just as pleasant, and she replies to them -

In all around they can not see
Relics of hopes and joys o'ercast -
They have not learned to live, like me
On recollections of the past.

Can this mean that after her broken engagement she had at once given up all thoughts of marriage, and really taken refuge in the past rather than imagine a future? Even now she is only thirty-two.

By this date she was evidently well advanced in her plans to move. But where? Another sonnet, written in the autumn, mourns over her beloved garden, growing wintry now. By the time it re-awakes to spring and the first primrose, she will be far, far away. Her well-off Burrard relations seem to have made no offers at this time of crisis: neither Calshot nor Walhampton could be said to be far away.

Though always delicate in health, at this time of double loss, Caroline showed her spirit. What were the prospects for a gentlewoman left destitute in the early nineteenth century? Lower class women went on the streets or became servants in big houses. About the only opening for a woman of Caroline's education was to become a governess, but one can not imagine her physical health or nerves standing up to that. With great courage she decided to maintain herself, and of course, *Ma Bonne* by her pen. Having so decided, she did not know how to go about getting her work published: Lymington offered little in the way of literary society. Always diffident about the value of her own work, she cast about for someone who could give her advice, and remembered the case of Henry Kirke White, the Nottingham boy whose poetry had made him famous.

Born a year earlier than herself, the son of a butcher, Henry had determined to be a writer when very young. He started work as a weaver, then managed to better himself as a lawyer's clerk, meanwhile sending out poems to literary magazines such as the *Monthly Mirror* with the hope of getting to Cambridge. When his first volume of poems was published, the *Monthly Review* called it "undistinguished boyish verse", but Henry sent a copy to one Robert Southey, who with his usual kindly enthusiasm took a keen interest in the boy's work. Henry reached his goal in 1805, entering St John's College, but died of tuberculosis the following year. No one today has ever heard of Henry, but his family sent all his manuscripts to Southey, who subsequently published *The Remains of Henry Kirke White*, with an account of his life. All this was ten years before. Caroline remembered the editor's name because the book had sold astonishingly well, going through ten editions.

So she resolved to send some of her work to Robert Southey, who had been made Poet Laureate in 1813, to see if he would give her any encouragement. What could she send? For the first time in her life, Caroline had to equate writing with money - short poems would not do, for she was aiming at book publication, no less. This was perhaps a pity, since some of her shorter lyrics and sonnets were of high quality. Going for length, she sent *Ellen Fitzgerald*, and on April 25th, 1818, wrote a long letter to Robert Southey, thereby altering the whole course of her life.

"I am startled at my own temerity, in venturing to approach Mr. Southey with a request which yet emanates from the very reverse of a presumptuous feeling - with a request that he will charitably devote some leisure hour to the perusal of the manuscript which accompanies this petition."

She goes on to relate the death of her mother, the loss of income and probably her home at some length, then continues - "Forgive me sir, for intruding on your time and patience the insignificant concerns of an obscure stranger; but I am tempted to believe Mr. Southey will not listen with a stranger's ear to the real, though common affliction of a fellow being, and I hope that this short detail will enable him to appreciate the motives of my conduct . . . I almost suspect that I have mistaken for natural taste a strong inclination for poetry, which has ruled me from childhood, possibly originating in the solitary reveries and pursuits incident to a very secluded life. I have never possessed the advantage of being acquainted with any person of literary habits; I have never even had access to a tolerable library and my life so stationary in this tame though beautiful country, in a neighbourhood where the society, though large, is most uninteresting, that my imagination is probably coloured with these surrounding tints and quite unable to aspire at any delineation beyond that of home scenes familiar to me from infancy.

And now what more can I say, but that I throw myself upon your indulgence? . . .

At all events, I feel assured that Mr. Southey's humanity and gentleness of heart will not suffer him to repulse contemptuously what his candour and judgement may oblige him, to condemn."

It is really a very long letter to write to a stranger - typed out it would take up at least three sides of A4 paper - a measure of Caroline's loneliness at this time, compelling her to pour out almost her life story, "with the ardent but fearful hope of gaining to myself a friend."

chapter three

A bird from an Eastern land

Who was this man to whom Caroline had written so confidingly? Robert Southey, born in Bristol in 1774, the son of a linen draper, was sent as a small child to live with his step-aunt, Elizabeth Tyler, an eccentric and imperious lady, passionate about the theatre, who lived in Bath, and took Robert to his first play when he was four. Later she introduced him to Shakespeare and to history, while her literary friends gave him books of poetry which he devoured even then with the same huge enjoyment he was to bring to books all his life. No wonder then that he was soon trying to write plays and poems of his own.

Since the linen drapery business did not flourish, and there were three sons younger than Robert, it was fortunate that his uncle, the Rev. Hubert Hill, chaplain to the British community in Lisbon, took over his education and sent him to Westminster School, where he made many friends and worked hard, thought to be destined for Oxford and the Church. But when an anonymous article appeared in the school magazine proclaiming flogging was the work of the Devil, the authorities were infuriated. When it was traced to Robert, he was expelled.

However, he did get to Oxford, learning chiefly, he said, to row and swim. When his father died, his mother moved to Bath, so that in vacations he was able to look up old friends there, including the Fricker sisters, Sara, Edith, Mary, Martha and Eliza. He was unhappy at Balliol, constantly worried by lack of money and a growing conviction that he could not subscribe to the Thirty Nine Articles as he must do in order to enter the Church of England, so that when a visitor from Cambridge, the rebel and brilliant speaker Samuel Taylor Coleridge erupted into his life, he was all too ready to abandon Oxford and join his scheme for emigrating to America. Robert was thoroughly unsettled: he had just become engaged to Edith Fricker and his first slim volume of poetry had recently been published jointly with his friend Robert Lovell.

Southey and Coleridge each recognised a kindred spirit. They began to share lodgings, to write poetry together and to plan Pantisocracy, their ideal community on the banks of the Susquehanna River. Edith, her sisters and Robert's mother were to be some of the twelve ladies to accompany twelve gentlemen. Enthusiasm knew no bounds. When Southey's Aunt Tyler discovered the scheme, she turned him out of the house in the middle of a thunderstorm! He also quarrelled with Coleridge at this time.

But it was really lack of money which dampened down the fires of enthusiasm, though they were to gutter on for some time. Meanwhile, Southey's very patient Uncle Hubert Hill invited him to Lisbon. Pausing only to marry Edith and find her a home with his bookseller friend, Cottle, he set off for Portugal. Under his uncle's scholarly eye, he threw himself with characteristic eagerness into the study of all things Portuguese.

On his return, he and Edith moved to London where he was to study law and where he could at last meet the celebrities of the day, including Charles Lamb, the painter William Opie, William Godwin and Mary Wollstonecraft. Robert began to contribute regularly to the *Morning Post*. His long poem, *Joan of Arc*, had been published while he was abroad. With this encouragement, he spent all his spare time in writing, while Coleridge went off to Germany on a long tour.

He had married Southey's sister-in-law, Sara Fricker, and on his return the two families were reconciled, Southey and Coleridge writing a poem together, *The Devil's Walk*. Soon after another stay in Portugal, Robert was back in London, but while acknowledging its usefulness to the literary career, he hated living there. After his first child Margaret was born, he and Edith moved to Westbury, then explored Wales, and returned to Bristol totally unsettled and grieving for Margaret who had lived only a year.

Robert was twenty eight and in spite of his false starts, already well known as a writer, author of several volumes of short poems, the epic *Thalaba*, his first book on Portugal, together with many reviews and essays in the literary magazines of the times. His knowledge of Portugal and its language brought him further work as translator and reviewer. Apart from Margaret's death, his marriage to Edith was happy and enduring. All they lacked was a proper home.

Then life was totally changed by an invitation to Greta Hall.

Coleridge with his wife Sara, their infant daughter, also Sara, and Mary Lovell, a recently widowed Fricker sister, had moved into this large house near Keswick, owned and still partly occupied by William Jackson and his housekeeper Mrs Wilson. It had a wonderful view over Skiddaw with mountains all about and stood within walking distance of the Wordsworths at Dove Cottage - Coleridge and Wordsworth were already being spoken of as the Lake Poets.

So the Southeys came to visit Greta Hall and found their home at last, the three sisters happy to be together again under one roof, Robert delighted with the scenery, the peaceful mountains and a settled home where he could at last arrange his vast library of books and manuscripts. The wetness of winter was conducive to settling down to write, while summer brought visitors from London or Bristol with all the latest literary news and gossip.

At that time there were three Coleridge children, Hartley aged eight, Derwent, four and Sara, two. Coleridge himself left soon after the Southey's arrival, escaping the bleak northern winter to work in Malta.

Soon Edith May Southey was born, later to be joined by Herbert, Emma, Bertha, Katherine, Isabel and after a long gap, Charles Cuthbert - a houseful of children and also of cats.

Soon the Wordsworths and Southeys were exchanging visits. In 1805, Captain John Wordsworth, William's brother, was drowned off Portland Bill, and Dorothy Wordsworth wrote in her diary, "Robert was so tender and kind that I loved him all at once - he wept with us in our sorrow and for that cause I think I must always love him."

By 1809 Southey had taken over the lease of Greta Hall. John Murray was just starting up the *Quarterly Review* - London's answer to the *Edinburgh Review*, and asked Southey to become a regular contributor. Over the years this was to be his lifeline, a constant source of income: even then with the whole household to run, he often found himself working far into the night. He also taught the children and in no small way, for young Sara Coleridge was to become a scholar and translator in her own right. He made time to carry on a voluminous correspondence with old friends from school and college, and new writers such as Landor and Shelley.

In 1813, Walter Scott was offered the post of Poet Laureate, but declined it as he already held two government appointments, and wrote a letter warmly commending Southey in his place, a characteristically generous gesture.

Their baby Emma only survived a short time, but a worse tragedy struck the Southeys in 1816 when their specially beloved and only son Herbert died, aged ten. Robert plunged into travel and work, including a monumental history of Brazil. By 1818, he was writing volume two, together with a life of Wesley.

So here is Robert Southey, sitting in his study with its view of the lakeland mountains, working steadily to maintain this large household, educating his four daughters and turning out dutiful odes for royal occasions for his ninety pounds a year Laureate salary, a man of great cheerfulness and laughter in spite of his difficult life and all the sorrows he had known. He is much travelled, a brilliant linguist, a loving father and husband, his every moment filled with writing, research, correspondence, the children, entertaining friends, striding over the fells to the Wordworths - and into his hands comes a letter and a long poem from a stranger, Caroline Bowles.

Caroline's letter has taken over a month to reach Keswick: it is a measure of his ready sympathy that he drops everything and replies at once, guessing her anxiety at so long a wait.

Keswick, May 28th 1818

This day and not till this day, did I receive your manuscript and the very interesting letter by which it was introduced. You will have expected to hear from me 'ere this, and I think I know how you will have thought and felt, as a suspicion has arisen of something even less pardonable than the brutal sort of repulse which you have done me the justice not to anticipate. Parcels lie for me at Messrs Longmans till they have occasion to send to me; they then travel by wagon, which owing to the risk of carriers, is a business of eighteen days or sometimes three weeks. Your packet has been fortunate in not having been longer in Paternoster Row.

I reply to your letter without the delay of a single post and with sincere pleasure; for though what I have to say may in some degree discourage hope, in all other respects it will correspond entirely to your wishes. The "Caroline Bowles, to whose very name and existence I was a stranger" this morning, cannot now be to me an "insignificant" person, one whom I shall soon forget or by whom I would willingly be forgotten.

Booksellers are not the most liberal or amiable of men. They are necessarily tradesmen. Of those whom I have any dealings, Murray is the one who would be least unlikely to risk the publication of your poem and the most likely to make the publication answer. He would perhaps take the risk upon himself and give you half the eventual profits. Shall I write to him upon the subject? Poor as these terms may appear, they are the best I have ever obtained for myself. My recommendation ought to have some weight with him.

I do not like such poems, because I am old enough to avoid all unnecessary pain. Real griefs do not lessen the suscepiblity for fictitious ones, but they take away all desire for them. There is a great deal of beauty in it - a womanly fluency, a womanly sweetness, a womanly truth and tenderness of feeling, which I have enough of my mother in me perfectly to understand. It is provoking to think that if the same powers had been displayed in prose instead of verse, in a novel instead of a poem, there would have been little or no doubt of finding a publisher; for supply of novels be what it will, the demand is sure to outrun it.

Many years ago I resided for a short time within ten miles of Lymington. I wish I were near enough now to see and converse with you. It is in planning a work that advice is useful. But to the point: if you think proper, I will write to Murray and ask him whether he will publish it; this I would wish you to consider as extremely doubtful, but if the application fails, it will not be for any want of warmth or sincerity in the recommendation. And if it should fail, you must not be discouraged, but turn your thoughts to something else, in prose or verse, in which, if I can assist you with any advice or direct you to any subjects which carry with them some attraction, I shall be very happy to show you that you have not honoured with your confidence one who is unfeeling, and therfore unworthy of it. For the present farewell, and believe me,

Yours, with sincere regard,

Robert Southey.

The warmth and concern in this first letter touched Caroline's lonely heart deeply: she was moved to write three months later, "While I live I shall never forget your kindness to me, at a season when kindness and gentleness is most soothing to a wounded spirit."

Now there is an incredible intervention in Caroline's life, like something from a fairy-tale. Into the midst of all her anxieties about money, having to uproot herself from beloved Buckland and establishing herself in a literary career, comes a letter from Persia [Iran]

It is from a Captain Bruce, who claims to be her brother! He is her father's adopted son and he is rich. Somehow her distressed circumstances have reached his ears. She wrote to Robert, "All of a sudden, as if from another world, started out to my assistance my father's adopted son, Mr Bruce, then resident at Bushire, [Bushehr, on the Persian Gulf] flourishing in splendid affluence. I think you know that in consequence of his vehement persuasions I remained on in this place, giving up those more prudent and then feasible plans which were already begun upon and that to enable me to do so, he gave me an annuity of one hundred pounds a year, a very small part of what he would have obliged me to accept had I wanted principle and delicacy so much as to accept more than was barely sufficient to enable me to live here with respectability."

One can not help but wish Caroline had not been so 'delicate' - had let herself go and accepted whatever this new brother would have heaped upon her: he *had* offered part of his fortune. To see the amount she chose in some sort of perspective, an agricultural labourer's pay was round twelve shillings a week, while an admiral's widow would be granted a pension of one hundred and twenty pounds a year. Caroline would still need some income from her writing. Captain Bruce was evidently delighted to have found a sister and was to suggest from time to time "sending me over an elephant or a dromedary or some such gigantic beast or bird from his Eastern land. Think how I was like to have been mounted."

So she could settle back once more in the cottage so webbed with memories of the past. Perhaps a move would actually have forced her to live in the present, consider the future, make a new life for herself. Now, as before, her days pass in writing, drawing, gardening, riding out on her pony and supervising her household, *Ma Bonne*, a maid and an elderly German gardener. She was often called upon, as single women are, to tend sick relatives and friends. Captain Bruce kept in touch with her, a warm, comic presence in a far country. Though as Robert had feared, Murray did reject *Ellen Fitzarthur*, Longman's accepted it, so her quality of life was improving. Above all there is her correspondence with Robert Southey which had already come to mean so much.

Thanks to her adoptive brother, she could afford occasional holidays now, and in the spring of 1819 went to Clifton, near Bristol, high above the rocky Avon Gorge, for her health. In the nineteenth century there was of course a great deal of travelling about - among the upper classes - in search of health, to spas such as Bath and Matlock, to mountains, or the coast, for bathing and sea breezes, a fashion promoted by George III. From Clifton she wrote to Robert asking if he could read the beginning of a long poem about her childhood - this was eventually to be called *The Birthday* and is the best of all her work. Robert had suggested that she should write a poem about the New Forest, but she had turned the subject down, rather surprisingly, saying she knew insufficient about it. He had also encouraged her to write a novel, to which she replied, "Poor as are my powers of composition in verse, I should find it still more difficult to write in prose: and a novel! I could as easily compose a treatise on chemistry." When he tried to lead her towards the consideration of more cheerful subjects, she wrote back, "I entirely agree with you: we need not create to ourselves fictitious griefs, but the mind recently afflicted colours everything with its own sadness. I wrote under such impressions, oppressed besides by languor of a very trying nervous disorder." So in spite of her deep respect for Robert as a writer, she does not always agree with him.

"Your letter has imparted to me the most pleasurable I have known for many a day. How much I wish you were indeed near enough for me to see and converse with you. Such a neighbourhood would give a new interest to my existence; but I live in a desert, of which, however, my little house is still the green valley."

The very name Clifton conjures up Robert's childhood and he replies, "Bristol is my native place and the first imagery which I ever drew from nature was from the rocks and woods about Clifton. There was (and probably still is) not far from Cook's Folly, a horse block upon the down, close to the vale - a point from whence a stranger looks down upon the river and the opposite woods; immediately under that horse block is a little cave, overhung with ivy, the access to which I should probably find difficult now; but, when I was between fifteen and eighteen, many and many are the verses which I wrote in that cave. One of my school fellows seemed at that time to have an inclination for poetry almost as decided as my own - we called ourselves Nisus and Euryalus, and the former of these names I cut in the rock where I used to take my seat."

In the same letter he asks her to send her blank verse to the home of his doctor brother in London, where he is going to stay.

At this time she had only written the first few hundred lines of *The Birthday*, which was eventually to take up ninety closely printed pages in her *Collected Poems*. One more birthday causes her to recall others in the past: Book One opens with a striking simile -

> As wayworn pilgrim on the last hill-top
> Lingers awhile, and, leaning on his staff,
> Looks back upon the pleasant plain o'erpassed,
> Retracing far, with retrospective eye,
> The course of every little glancing stream
> And winding valley path...

> ... that wayfaring man
> Leans on his staff and looks a long farewell
> To all the lovely land: So linger I,
> Life's lonely Pilgrim, on the last hill-top,
> With thoughtful, tender, retrospective gaze,
> Ere, turning down the steep descent I go,
> Of the cold shadowy side.

Robert replied with his usual energy and enthusiasm. "I read your manuscript this morning and will rather dispatch a hasty letter than let a post elapse without telling you of its arrival and exhorting you, by all means to proceed with the poem. It is a very sweet strain: go on with it, and you will produce something which may hold a permanent place in English Literature ... The flow of verse is natural and the language unconstrained. Everyone will recognise the truth of the feeling which produces it, and there is a charm in the pictures, the imagery and the expression which cannot fail to be felt."

Robert had just returned from a trip to Scotland and is planning to visit London for the publication of his *Life of Wesley*.

"I am too busy at present to say more; only understand these hurried lines as encouraging you in the strongest and most unequivocal manner to proceed"

Caroline wrote in January, 1820, "Encouraged thus by you, I cannot but proceed with it and indeed the subject is such that I should loath to leave ... I wish that when you read the manuscript you had drawn your pen unsparingly through such parts as appeared to you most objectionable. There is a chance that I may be in London, on my way, (a circuitous one) to Worcestershire. I look forward with apprehension to that possibility, for no pleasant business awaits me in the great city; but I should be in some measure reconciled to the painful cause which may draw me there, could I hope then to become personally acquainted with Mr Southey."

So, at last Caroline and Robert arranged to meet, in Chelsea.

chapter four

Dear and kind friend of mine

It was a pity that Robert was in a hurry: this may have added to Caroline's nervousness. He was to write afterwards, "I wish I could have seen you again at Chelsea, but my very minutes were numbered while I was in and about London, nor did I ever feel anything like a sense of rest from the time I entered it till I got into the mail coach on my return."

The man she was to meet was forty six, very tall and slim, with curly black hair, penetrating hazel eyes and 'a remarkable habit of looking up into the air as if at abstractions, with an air of distance and reserve about him.' The previous year Edith had borne a son, Cuthbert, who, while never taking the place of Herbert, had done much to cheer his heart.

Caroline naturally felt excited at meeting the man she had now corresponded with for two years, and was ready to show herself equally interested in his work. A friend wrote of her, "Besides being agreeable herself, she had the rare talent of making everyone she wished to please feel agreeable too. No one more readily caught a friend's idea, but it was quite a chance whether she would hold it up in a comical light or with a variety of shades from her own fancy." But she caught none of his ideas, was so overcome by the sight of Robert in the flesh as to be struck dumb with shyness and quite unable to thank him as she had meant to do for all the detailed criticism he had given her over *Ellen Fitzarthur*.

Sending him a copy of this a few days later from Chelsea, she wrote, "I offer it with the thankful acknowledgement that, faulty as the poem still is, it would have been much more so but for Mr Southey's advice and critical remarks. Let me thank you, my dear sir, more intelligibly than I could do *viva voce*, for your goodness in coming to see me at this place: to confess the truth, I derive more pleasure from the reflection that I am become acquainted with you than I did at the actual making of that acquaintance, for then I found that all I meant and wished to say was clean vanished, and that I had only your charity (and penetration perhaps) to trust to for not setting me down as an ungrateful and insensible idiot. It is not with me that 'out of the abundance of the heart the mouth speaks.'"

She returned home angry at herself at being so overcome with shyness, but looking forward to her continued correspondence with Robert.

But when she reached Buckland, there was no letter waiting. Later, she sent a further instalment of *The Birthday*, then some poems on the death of George III, then a drawing of Bristol, Robert's native town, made while she was staying at Clifton. Yet autumn passed without a word from Keswick. She was working on a new narrative poem, *The Widow's Tale* and trying out her hand at prose, as Robert had suggested this might be easier to get published. By Christmas there was still no word and Caroline, always ready to blame herself, feared that actually seeing her had put Robert off ever communicating with her again. She kept remembering how gauche and tongue-tied she must have appeared at their meeting.

No wonder then that she was depressed and ill 'with a low fever' for much of the winter, unable to concentrate on writing anything, huddling behind the walls of Buckland Cottage, looked after by her old nurse. For all her ladylike appearance, Caroline was very much an outdoor woman: bad winter weather which prevented her rambles, pony rides and gardening were always to depress her frail nerves, but this winter, without a word from Robert, was especially grim.

Why did Robert leave a gap of eight months? Had he sensed that Caroline was more fond of him than was seemly at their one short meeting, and allowed a cooling off period? Or was it just pressure of work, as he assured her, with innumerable visitors and letters. "One man asks for an acrostic for his mistress and another consults me upon a scheme to pay off the National Debt!"

At last, with the first stirrings of spring, a drift of snowdrops in the garden and the earliest daffodils, Caroline received - not one letter, but two. "I have been intending and intending to write to you ever since my return home in July and more especially since I got your poem in November. But you know what becomes of good intentions!" He goes on to describe all the comings and goings at Greta Hall, then mentions a good review of *Ellen Fitzarthur* in *New Monthly*. "Your stanzas upon the king's death are very good, both in thought, feeling and expression. Go on with your blank verse poem *The Birthday*, the subject will secure for it a favourable acceptance, relating as it does to feelings which find sympathy in every kind heart." He promised that Longman's, his publishers would send her his own latest work shortly. This was also on the death of George III, a poem called *A Vision of Judgement*, which was to be parodied by Byron and cause much literary feuding.

So far the letter had been much as usual, partly about his affairs, partly to encourage her writing, but the last paragraph was what really mattered to Caroline.

"You and I must be better acquainted personally: you must become acquainted with my wife and daughters. One spare room will be filled this summer; but next year we shall be very glad if you will let us show you this neighbourhood, if we may dare to look on so long."

Had Robert decided that it would be too unkind to cut Caroline's romantic yearnings out of his life altogether, so she had best come and see him as he really was, a loyal family man? Or is that too subtle? Had Robert simply been desparately busy and now feeling guilty for not having written, wanted to cheer her up? Never mind, the invitation was there, even though for next year - he had not forgotten her after all. She started sowing seeds in the garden. With the letter was enclosed a note penned the next day, thanking her for the sketch of Clifton and ending up - "I please myself in thinking about what a pleasure you will have in sketching here, where, if you have never been fairly in a mountainous country, you will find yourself almost in a new world."

So once more she can write to Robert certain of a friendly reply. She tells him how a low fever has prevented her writing, of a small fire that broke out at Buckland Cottage, that her biographical poem has now doubled in length and that she has collected up her miscellaneous pieces in an anthology which she hopes Longman's may publish - before going on to what really mattered.

"You hold out to me a gilded bait - yet not so - a delightful hope I should call it - if I dared look on to next year, next summer. To visit you in your own world of lakes and mountains! to become really acquainted with you, with your family! How I should long for such pleasure, if I had not almost left off longing for anything, if I dared look forward beyond the springing up or flowering of the annuals I am now sowing in my little flower garden. Sometimes, in a sunshiny mood of the mind, I say to myself, 'Well, but who knows? - perhaps -' and then I stop, and the wide interval of time and distance spreads drearily before me, not impossibly, however, and I will hope, for once."

In her last paragraph, Caroline stops wondering how long she has to live and asks baldly, "Is there any chance of your being in town this spring?" She has to travel there on business with nothing pleasant in hand except a viewing of the latest canvas by the artist Benjamin Robert Haydon. "Surely," she asks urgently, "you who have half a hundred other works in the press, must have business in London?"

No meeting came about that year, but in better spirits Caroline took up her writing again and sent some poems to Blackwood's, the

Edinburgh firm which published books as well as their famous magazine, thus making a new friend by correspondence in William Blackwood, who not only published her poems and paid her well for them, but also sent her parcels of new books, which were manna in the literary desert of Lymington.

On August 13th she wrote to her new editor, "Far from being offended by Mr Blackwood's liberal proposals, I see no reason I may not unhesitatingly accept such remuneration as he judges proportionate to the success of my literary attempts."

Later she thanks him for sending her Lockhart's *Spanish Ballads*, writing for the first time in this correspondence from Walhampton, the Burrard mansion, where she stayed for part of the following winter. Walhampton, with its high, spacious rooms, ornate plastered ceilings, pillared halls, terraces, lakes and formal gardens, all maintained by an army of servants, was a far cry from the small, cosy rooms of her cottage. The ghost of beautiful Laura Burrard, who had fallen dead on the eve of her wedding, was said to haunt one of the corridors: more bracingly there were wide views across the Solent and the gentle farming country round about. From here, Caroline sent Robert her second book, published, again anonymously, by Routledge.

The Widow's Tale is another narrative poem full of tragedy. Robert wrote, "Thank you for your little volume. Have I perused it with pleasure? Both with as much pleasure and as much pain as you have wished to excite. And whether most to find fault with you for choosing such deeply tragic subjects, or to praise you for the manner in which you have treated them, I know not.

For the execution, it is not too much to say that you have become such a poetess as I believed and hoped from the first. You have the ear and the heart and the eye of poetry and you have them in perfection."

But Robert had known great sorrow in his life, particularly in the deaths of his children, and was always to try and encourage Caroline towards more cheeful subjects, rather than add to the woes of the world. He goes on, "Give us, I entreat you, a picture in summer and sunshine - a tale that in its progress and termination shall answer the wishes of the reader. Make the creatures of your imagination as happy as you would make them if they were real beings, whose fortune depended upon your will; your poem will then be read again and again with delight. You will please more readers, and please them more. It is a road to popular favour which has not been tried in this country and it is a sure one. Goethe and Voss have found it so in Germany.

It is better for yourself too, to dwell upon happier themes; you have no such exuberance of health and spirits that you can afford with impunity to shed so many tears as these poems must have cost you."

This was to be an ongoing argument, Caroline maintaining that she could only write poetry when she was deeply moved, which was most often by tragedy, and secondly that such gloomy reading was what editors seemed to want anyway. But when her health allowed, she did continue with the long poem about her childhood, which is full of light-hearted moments.

One cheering event of the summer was the arrival of fan mail from another poet. William Lisle Bowles, vicar of Bremhill in Wiltshire, was a famous writer of his day, and though largely now forgotten, was a formative influence on Coleridge. Later, Robert was to descibe a visit to his parsonage, "There is a jet fountain and two swans, Snowdrop and Lily, who marched up to the breakfast room window to demand their food ... he is a delightful old gentleman, his oddity, his untidiness, his simplicity, his benevolence, his fears and his good nature make him one of the most entertaining and extraordinary characters I ever met."

William wrote to Robert, "You mention my namesake Caroline. If you write, do make my warmest congratulations known to her. Have I read *Ellen Fitzarthur*? There was only one copy in Bath; no one read a word of it; no one thought of buying it; no one spoke of it. I was the first in this neighbourhood to bring it into notice. I spoke to everyone with the utmost warmth of it, as deeply affecting in story and beautiful in genuine language of poetry. I trumpeted it to Lord and Lady Lansdowne, Miss Fox, and all the literati of Bowood; and, without knowing the name, I flatter myself I contributed in some degree to its more general notice among some distinguished ornaments of taste and literature. I should be happy to know Caroline, and more to think of her a relation. I think a poem so remote from the golden-silvery-diamond-alabaster-Pontypool-style of the present Cockney race of dandy poetasters cannot be too much noticed; and I am rejoiced the real touches of nature and passion have awakened attention." In a postscript, he adds, "I think I shall write a note to Caroline with my poem." Robert of course took great pleasure in relaying all this to Caroline, who had met the poet when she was a child.

She very soon received a most flattering letter from William, together with his latest book of poems. For the rest of his life, William was to claim her as a cousin and visit Buckland Cottage whenever near Lymington. "I wrote by today's post to thank him for his valuable and valued gift," she wrote to Robert. "But I have charged him with the fact of rejecting me as a kinswoman in days of yore, when - an aspiring little damsel - I was fain to claim relationship with the author of *The Sonnets*."

In his previous letter, Robert had signed off, "God bless you, sister poetess. I have a right to call you so, though I cannot look for a relationship like Bowles." Caroline replied, "Claim kindred with me as you will, I will gratefully admit the title." He had also asked in his kindly way, "How are you and what are you doing?" To which Caroline replied with the fullest description she ever gives of her state of health.

"How different a creature I might have been, of how much better things I might have been capable, had my earlier path in life been gilded with that degree of encouragement which now falls upon me - now, when my days on earth are so nearly numbered. Yes, I have been very ill, with repeated attacks in the head, each succeeding one increasing in seriousness and continuance, and yielding only to such violent remedies as shake almost to dissolution the fragile frame. This affection of the head, is, I am told, more symptomatic of general debility and consequent derangement of the nervous system, than in itself a primary complaint; but it is not on that account less terrible to endure. I had almost said it was worse than pain; but that would be a thankless, presumptous assertion. It is almost total loss of memory, a confusion of ideas, a deprivation of all comprehensive power, with such a darkness of spirit as would indeed 'turn my day into night' were it not for the one heavenly ray that pierceth all darkness. All this comes upon me accompanied by an apprehensive weight and giddiness, that, while it lasts, incapacitates me for all mental and bodily exertion, and the least attempt at the latter so accelerates the pulsation of the heart as to make every throb dreadfully distressing. So long an answer must I give to your simple question, 'How are you?'"

Though it is always difficult in diagnosing across two hundred years, medical opinion considers that she probably suffered from a severe and recurrent form of migraine.

Perhaps it was for health reasons that her projected visit to Keswick did not take place that year, but the following summer she was well enough to set out on a long jaunt, after a spring spent working on her first prose collection, *Chapters on Churchyards*. She stayed first of all in Oxford, then for three weeks in Leamington Spa to take the waters, then at last the coach dropped her at Keswick.

Greta Hall stands alone on a wooded hillock above a sweeping bend of the river Greta, looking out over the world from three rows of tall windows - the very opposite of hidden Buckland. The view from its windows had made Coleridge exclaim, "Right before me is a camp of single mountains - each in shape resembles a giant's tent and to the left is the lake of Keswick, with its islands and white sails and glossy lights of evening . . . the three remaining sides are encircled by the most fantastic mountains that ever earthquakes made in sport." So Caroline arrived at this house which had been visited by many of the leading writers of her time, young Shelley with his new bride, De Quincey, Walter Scott, Charles Lamb, and most frequently, Wordsworth and his sister Dorothy.

Once inside the pillared doorway, Caroline was greeted by a bewildering number of people. William Jackson, a local builder and bachelor, still lived at the back with his housekeeper Mrs Wilson who had also acted as nannie to the children. Hartley and Derwent were now in their twenties and away, but Sara still lived at home, (educated by Robert) at twenty a beautiful and accomplished young woman, later to become a translator and writer. Her mother, also Sara, one of a large family of sisters, was a lively, totally unliterary gossip. Her marriage with Samuel Taylor Coleridge had fallen apart many years before: broken in health and addicted to the opium first prescribed for his health, her husband was living in Highgate, with his doctor, James Gillman. Her sister, Mary Lovell, widowed when very young, lived with the Coleridges, and a third Fricker sister, Edith, was Robert's wife.

Then there were the Southey children, Edith-May, who was nineteen, Bertha, fourteen, Kate thirteen, Isabel, known as Belle, eleven, and the afterthought, Cuthbert, who was four and passionate about cats.

What with the long journey, the strange wild mountain country and this household of a dozen people, Caroline must have retired to bed that first night exhausted, bewildered and generally overwhelmed, but happy to be under the same roof as Robert.

Caroline was thirty seven, in age the odd one out. She did not seem to make friends with the younger women, Sara or Edith-May, for they did not correspond after the visit and Kate took a dislike to her, even then. The older women were busy about the house and little interested in a visiting writer. She did find common ground with Mary Lovell who was a keen gardener. It was Cuthbert and his cats who became her immediate friends. She would take him aside and tell him cat stories, while together they would invent more fearsome cat names - already one was called Rumplestilzchen and another, Tchitchigoff. In later letters there were often whimsical cat-notes to be passed on to Cuthbert, while his father was to relay such vital news as Cuthbert's first pair of breeches, though his four daughters seldom get a mention.

What did Edith Southey think of Caroline's visit? It lasted more than a month. Hartley Coleridge has left an interesting picture of his aunt. "Never knew I a being in whom a pure and benevolent spirit was so little joyous; a morbid sensitiveness to pain and an almost apathy to pleasure, an intellect sensible and not uncultivated, but of little activity." Hartley had lived in the same house with her from childhood, so knew Aunt Edith well, but one must allow for the entirely male point of view. She had borne eight children and was largely responsible for the domestic running of this extensive household though there were servants to help. This would have left her little time for intellectual activity, though it freed Robert for the long hours in his study. Most important of all in considering her character, she had lost three of those children, including precious ten year old Herbert, then her only son. No wonder she was 'so little joyous.' Perhaps she felt too secure in Robert's love and as mother of his large family, to be jealous: visitors had come and gone for years. Various letters and memoirs of the time describe the ménage at Greta Hall, as busy, bustling, lively or happy - she was at the heart of it.

But her deep love for Robert was for himself: his work was largely outside her interest, something he must do to maintain the family. Miss Bowles however was a published poet, able to enter into literary discussions with Robert as Edith never did.

For much of the time Robert was busy in his first floor study with its arched windows and view across Keswick to the fells, working on his voluminous history of the Peninsular Wars, writing reviews and trying to keep up with his vast correspondence. He did find time to pose for Caroline outside the front door of Greta Hall and though he is only a distant figure, seen through the trees she exactly catches his extreme slenderness which gave him a boyish figure even at the age of nearly fifty.

Indoors there was always a hum of conversation, frequent visitors, and Robert's vast library. One of the visitors was Dora Wordsworth, a close friend of Edith-May and Sara Coleridge, who was later to send Caroline books.

It did rain rather a lot so that they never had the planned walk to Watendlath, but with or without Robert there were all kinds of visits and excursions that September among the lakes and hills, to Honister Crag, Friar's Crag, the lake shore. One such is described by Caroline's friend, E.O. "On an exquisite summer's day, a party had been got up by the young people who had themselves prepared the meal that was spread now by the falls of Lodore. Sara Coleridge, then in the bloom of her ethereal beauty, had made a basketful of remarkably nice cakes. Caroline sketched her and all the group." The sketch, which included Dora Wordsworth was later lithographed and entitled *A Picnic among the Hills*, so one can check on E.O.'s information and know it to be true.

Apparently it is not always so, for she goes on to say, "Wordsworth with more time than Robert became her guide and used to walk for miles beside her pony, pointing out every fold of hills with their glens and tarns. Scarcely a shadow from the passing clouds swept across lake or upland pasture without his remarking it. He was fond of repeating his own poetry in illustration of the scenery in a strong, north country accent and very sonorous tone."

While this is a striking picture and sounds very like Wordsworth, Caroline was to write in her first letter to Robert after the holiday, "Just as we reached Rydal that evening, Mr Wordsworth himself and all his family I believe, came to meet the coach, and waited long beside it, while some parcel in which they were in expectation of was searched for, during all of which time I very wisely shrank back in my corner, instead of bowing to Mr Wordsworth, as I ought to have done, having been introduced to him in your house."

This hardly sounds as if the pony rambles could be true, whereas in her letters to Robert for months to come, there are references to excursions which they had together or with the family. "I often shut my eyes and see myself standing with you on the point of Friar's Crag to which we walked so frequently. I see the fretwork pavement as plain as when I stood upon it: the crags and stones beneath: the red boles of the tall firs, through which we looked up towards the grand pass into Borrowdale and that conical mountain that stood like a sentinel at its entrance, always more darkly blue than its surrounding brethren."

And it was Robert himself who sometimes declaimed his own poetry when they were out among the lakes and mountains and even burst into song, though he confessed not to know one note from another, claiming that when other people sang up to G, he went on to X,Y,Z! In the twilight among the echoes of Borrowdale, he sang, *The Bloody Gardener*, and at Waterend a pathetic ditty called *Tittymouse Bay.*

So it was a holiday full of rambles and picnics and company. When it rained, Caroline explored Robert's library or sketched his study, the heart of his life.

Parting was painful. She looked back from the coach at mountains dark against the sky as if they were the gates of Robert's Eden, had even lingered at an inn near Rydal hoping the sun might shine once more upon the tops, but was rewarded only with a thunder storm echoing grandly round the peaks.

After all the excitements and bustle of Greta Hall, Buckland must have seemed incredibly quiet, though one can detect a certain relief in her thank you letter to Robert. "On Wednesday evening I stepped once more over the threshold of my quiet little house and was welcomed by my dear nurse with such a welcome as those only can bestow to whom we are objects of exclusive affection. Dogs, cats and pony all in their several fashions testified great joy at the sight of me . . . To each and every member of your happy circle I send greeting warm and grateful." She had so much enjoyed getting to know his family and himself, sent a special message from her cat Donna to Cuthbert and ends, "have I not the privilege of calling you friend."

Writing to Robert was quite different now because she could picture him amongst his family in the tall grey house with its unusual, semi-circular wings and its panoramic views of Borrowdale, Skiddaw and Derwentwater. Yet it must have hurt to see how much he belonged to other people. During that month, had she fallen in love with Robert? Starved of any other relationship with a man, then suddenly included in Robert's warm concern for all those about him and moreover able to talk over with him her deeply personal writing, it would be strange if she had not. But the strict morality of her upbringing would not allow her to recognise love for a married man: any thought of breaking up Robert's happy marriage would have been totally alien - even outside her wildest imagination, since she always held herself in low esteem.

Nothing in her writing gives any clue as to her state of mind on returning home. Certainly there was no burst of love lyrics or stories - she is busy writing *Chapters on Churchyards*, not a title which would seem to herald a new beginning.

One thought buoyed her up: before she left Keswick, they had arranged that Robert should come and stay at Buckland on one of his journeys south.

Robert was far less repressed. He quickly wrote her a letter full of affection, signed Dear friend, farewell. "I am heartily glad that you have reached home safely, and with so few disagreeables on the way, that the fear of such a journey will not stand in the way of repeating it; for I will not believe that you have taken leave of these mountains for ever. You must not talk of sunset pleasures yet. Your evening is far distant; and many such pleasures as this country can afford are in store I hope, for both you and for me. If you are half as desirous of partaking them again as I am that you should do so, the difficulties in the way will only be thought of with the view to overcoming them. Whatever we may think of dreams, you will allow that daydreams may have some truth in them and you have borne no small part in mine since your departure. These at least may bring about their accomplishment.

On the day you reached Oxford, we effected our Watendlath excursion. Go whither I will among these lakes and mountains, I have more ghosts than Sir Thomas More to accompany me; there is scarcely a spot but brings with it some indelible recollection of those whom I have loved and lost. But the predominant feeling on this day was regret that you were not with us." That was a sentence to warm Caroline's heart. He went on to describe his itinery in coming south to London. "From thence you shall hear of my movements. I have a wide way to travel and the sunniest spot in the prospect is the New Forest."

There follows some nonsense about Cuthbert's cat newly created a marquis and the letter concludes, "I am charged also to send Rumpel's love to Donna and Cuthbert's to you. There are remembrances moreover from each and all of my womenkind, with all of whom you have left such an impression as you would desire to leave. For myself - but I must have done, for time presses and the maid is waiting for my dispatches."

The women's greetings seem a trifle enigmatic as if Robert is making the best of them, a presage of things to come. But his own feelings are hardly hidden by that hasty dash at the end - he obviously holds Caroline in considerable affection. His letters, after that previous long silence, become much more frequent, even though he was so involved in literary affairs. Charles Lamb, an erstwhile friend, had attacked him in

The London Journal: Lord Byron had written his wickedly brilliant parody of Robert's poem on the death of George III, *A Vision of Judgement*. When Caroline commiserates with him, he shrugs off such criticisms with superb good humour. "When I have found it necessary to take up the pen against Lord Byron, it has been more with a feeling of strength than of anger, something like Rumpelstilzchen feels when he lays his paw upon a rat."

Buckland's gentle woods and pastures may have seemed tame country after the dramatic views from Greta Hall - but they were not so. Just along the road was an inn (now called the *Toll Gate*) from which a tunnel led up into the grounds of Buckland Cottage: this was used by local smugglers as part of their route to and from the river in the valley just below. Caroline never mentions the tunnel itself, but it was obviously the reason why her garden and its immediate neighbourhood were often traversed by noisy nocturnal gangs.

On October 27th she wrote to Robert, "I have had a rude welcome home. The very night after I wrote to you my little lonely dwelling was beset by a complete gang of thieves, whose attack was fortunately confined to the outer premises: there they made unsparing havoc, tearing down and taking away (in a cart brought for the purpose) everything at all portable - harness, tools, lead-work, etc., and what they could not carry off they broke or cut to pieces. So well aware were these depredators of the weakness of the garrison, that they by no means constrained themselves to work in silence, for about twelve o'clock I distinctly heard many voices of persons round the house. Like a fool however I lay still and went to sleep, instead of giving the alarm to my old German [the gardener] the report of whose musket out of the window might have scared away the robbers, but I am so accustomed to hear nocturnal disturbances occasioned by smugglers and poachers and have so often needlessly awakened the family, that this once the wolf came and robbed my fold in good earnest.

This is not to me the worst part of the disaster, though my loss is not inconsiderable; but the whole neighbourhood, having been lately kept in a state of alarm from the depredations of this gang, and just fears being entertained that with winter coming on they would not stop at outdoor robbery, the police set to work in the present case with such prompt activity as to ferret out four of the ringleaders, one only of whom they succeeded in securing with just enough of my property in his possession to fix on me the neccessity of prosecution."

The thought of this fills her with horror, since breaking open doors and windows could be a capital offence. However she is assured that hanging would be commuted to transportation for life to which she has no objection.

The letter continues, "I am kindly comforted on all hands with hints that I may expect diverse malicious and revengeful acts from those of the gang still at liberty. Maiming of cattle, house-breaking, house-firing - all these pleasant anticipations are tenderly murmured in my ear, but happily produce in me the very reverse effect to what might be expected for, in the first place, I think myself in no manner of danger and have not allowed myself to be frightened out of an hour's sleep; and, in the next, am spirited up to defend myself bravely, and, like a good general, have already put my fortress in proper state to withstand siege.

First, by way of warning, I have stuck a huge, frightful engine y-clept a mantrap (not set at night, but you are not to blab that secret) then I have bought a great fierce bulldog; have provided my German with a blunderbuss, powder and shot, and myself with a pair of pistols, with which I dare make a noise at least; for you know I told you my father had taught me to stand fire, and the report (soon spread) that one has such weapons and dare use them, is almost as effective as an armed sentinel at one's door. Now dare you trust yourself in my 'little lonely tower?' But you dare not draw back, indeed, you have too much chivalric spirit about you; and I will not let you off - no, nor part with you a day, nor an hour, nor a minute sooner than you say must be the last."

Here is one of the delightful surprises of Caroline's character. Just when one had a clear image of a ladylike spinster fond of books and her flowers, here she is toting a pair of pistols and really rather enjoying coping with what was a potentially very frightening situation. Frail or no, she would always rise to the occasion.

At the end of the letter she suggests that Robert should bring some of his work with him, so that he can stay longer. "For quiet you shall have a little study so still it might answer for the cell of silence, and for hours, it shall be at your own disposal as in your own home; so come and work here." The letter went on to prescribe cream cheese paté for Rumpel's cough and ended, "Farewell for a season, dear kind friend of mine."

Robert wrote a quick comforting note in haste as he was about to leave for London, but two days later wrote with more leisure from Kirby Lonsdale. He had obviously been concerned about Caroline, worrying about her fits of depression and thinking out a plan which could only bring them closer together. "One of those daydreams to which you have given birth (a delightful one to me it is) shall come to pass.

I have put up among my papers the memoranda which were made many years ago for a poem on Robin Hood. These are easily shaped into a regular plan, and in my judgement, a promising one. Will you form an intellectual union with me that it may be executed? We will keep our own secret as well as Sir Walter Scott has done. Murray shall publish it and not know the whole mystery that he may make the more of it, and the result will be means in abundance for a summer's abode in Keswick and an additional motive for it that we may form schemes of the same nature. Am I dreaming when I think that we may derive from this much high enjoyment, and that you may see in the prospect something which is worth living for? The secret itself would be delightful while we thought proper to keep it; still more so the spiritual union which death would not part.

Now on your side there must be no hesitation from diffidence. You can write as easily and well as I can plan. You are as well acquainted with forest scenery and with whatever is required for the landscape part, as I am with the manners of the time. When we meet we will sort out the parts so as each to take the most suitable, and you will add to mine and I to yours whatever may improve it. Beaumont and Fletcher composed plays together with such harmony of style, thought and feeling that no critic has ever been able to determine what parts were written by one and what by the other. Why should not R.S. and C.A.B. succeed as happily in the joint execution of a poem?

As there can be no cause or just impediment why these two persons should not be joined together, tell me that you consent to the union and I will send you the rude outline of the story and the characters."

This letter with all it implies naturally threw Caroline into a state of joyful confusion. His warm concern for her is obvious: he wants her to come to Keswick again. He wants them joined in secret union - even using the words of the marriage service. She replied only to his offer of literary collaboration. Just the same, this called forth the most human and emotional letter yet, full of dashes rather than long stately sentences.

"How you have set me thinking! Thinking, wondering, wishing, debating, doubting, almost - yes, almost - despairing. What! I associated with you in any literary undertaking! I have dreamed often enough, and strangely enough Heaven knows, and have been (what I thought) daring in my dreams; but never in their very wildest flight glanced at such a possibility of such a scheme. That would be something worth living for, and rather would I be associated therein - yes, contribute thereto the very humblest, meanest portion, the very commas and semi-colons, thereby cementing that undying intellectual union you speak of - than be the authoress, the sole authoress of such a work as *Thalaba*. I can find no language to express more warmly how, with heart and soul, I would say 'Yes,' promptly and eagerly, 'Yes' - to your tempting, tantalizing proposition, if only - that odious monosyllable! You know well enough all it implies. You must know, if you consider by the cold clear light of reason alone, unmingled with the warm, illusive emanations from that kind heart of yours, which (in its zeal to make me in love with life) had conjured up all this beautiful fabric. But let it stand awhile; I have not the heart to demolish it with one resolute word. And 'what if I were to try' whispers the longing spirit within me; I could but fail at last, and there would be no harm done, and the friend who has conceived all this so delightfully would not withdraw his regard, nor think more meanly of me as a friend in the best sense of the word, because I fall on trial so immeasurably below him in the scale of intellectual worth. So whispers The Voice. Is it that of a friendly or foolish spirit? Answer my question by sending or not sending the outline you speak of. In feeling, I think, I believe, I may go along with you; but when I would express those feelings, even in familiar conversation, I feel myself hemmed in like a salamander in his glowing circle, baffled, obstructed, repelled in every quarter.

Moreover you know I have told you I cannot write ; I cannot sit down to compose; that would effectually discompose my scanty stock of ideas. Can you solve this difficulty? I know you can work wonders and are more than half a magician; so speak over me words of such power as may make me what you say I can be. In short, your 'daydreams' are so enchanting I must try to share in them a little while at the risk, the almost certainty, of awaking at last to a blank and mortifying reality ... Good angels speed you hither!"

Robert replied swiftly, from Norwich, with an outline of the story, for it was to be a long narrative poem, ending his letter, "How like you this, my friend and partner dear? Are there not rich capabilities to be dreamt of now - to be talked of soon - and then to be realised?"

So, in the middle of winter, having finished his business in London, Robert came to stay with Caroline at Buckland Cottage.

chapter five

A little bit of a virago

Tall, bare elms half encircled the long brick house and its rambling garden, shutting out the world: inside all was warmth and welcome. One of the first things to meet Robert's eye in Caroline's sitting room was a large drawing on the wall, of his own study and the opening of a new book box from London. Soon they were settled by the fire, deep in discussion of this delightful new plan, of writing a poem together, for though Caroline dithered over *Robin Hood*, she could not withstand Robert's enthusiasm.

"I dared not say yes, and I could not find it in my heart to say no. So the memoranda arrived and the rough sketch followed and in no time came the writer. Full of his project, full of kindness, of energy, of hope, he did his utmost to encourage and enspirit me, and his hopeful spirit was at least contagious for the time being."

What were Robert's motives for suggesting their collaboration? With his own brimming vitality and love of life, he certainly wanted to alleviate Caroline's fits of lonely despair when she talked only of death. But he seems also genuinely drawn to her, and the fact of their being literary partners would draw a veil of respectability over this visit and others to come.

Caroline gave Robert what no other woman had been able to offer, a deep interest and concern in his writing and literary life. For Caroline it was a great joy that six years after her first, shy letter to Robert, he should actually be sitting beside her in Buckland Cottage.

"We talked over *Robin Hood* by my quiet fireside, suggesting, objecting, altering, disputing (as it was pleasant to dispute) and when we came to the question of versification, the metre of Robert's ballad, *Thalaba* (for which, in an evil hour I had declared my preference) was selected on that account, despite my plea that to admire and to achieve were two very different things and that I was sure I should never succeed in it. My protests against anything to do with battle scenes and the like were more readily admitted and the women and children and forest were assigned to my management."

Robert had largely given up writing poetry at this time, in favour of long prose histories and bread-and-butter reviews, but he promised, as the days would soon grow lighter, to rise earlier on his return home and work on *Robin Hood*, this being the only writing time that he could spare. In the past he had written the narrative poems *Roderick, Kehama,* and *Thalaba* itself at this early hour.

It was a great pity that they decided on *Thalaba*, with its pattern of long and short lines. Caroline was still working on *The Birthday*, in blank verse which was her great strength. "I have been at work trying that metre of *Thalaba* and fine work I make of it ! It is to me just like trying to drive a tilbury in a tram road. I keep quartering for a yard or so and then down goes the wheel into the old groove. I cannot keep out of blank verse."

But they did not work at *Robin Hood* all the time. Caroline was a considerate hostess and put a small study aside for Robert's sole use so that he could keep up with his reviewing schedule, and refused to let him be disturbed by visitors. This set the pattern for future visits so that Robert was able to look forward to undisturbed working sessions at Buckland.

It was only a short visit. "So we parted, with a promise on my part to do my best - " Caroline slightly consoled by this new link between them which promised more letters and even visits. Soon after his departure came a surprise parcel which not only filled her with delight, but showed how much thought Robert put into the relationship. It was his collected poems in several volumes and each specially bound in green leather, an edition which must have been ordered some time before, with the first volume inscribed to her. "You should not have lavished on me that elegant binding, which I am determined not to let you know I think beautiful. With a few strokes of your pen you have made one volume more valuable to me than the whole art of binding could have rendered it."

During Robert's visit, all had been quiet in the neighbourhood, but these were troubled times: agricultural wages being reduced again led to widespread poaching. Recently there had been a pitched battle between gamekeepers and poachers near Winchester, a few miles to the north, and the terrible fear of starvation brought out mobs threatening to burn the new-fangled threshing machines which threatened the poorly paid jobs they *did* have. In the north, children as young as seven were packed off to work long hours in the textile mills, but news of this had not yet impinged on Caroline: when it did she was appalled, and took what action she could.

She was in fact very busy after Robert's departure. Though she often mentions her own inability to settle down to work for long periods, she had not only written *Ellen Fitzarthur*, and *The Widow's Tale* and become a valued contributor to Blackwood's Magazine. She had recently collected her poems and stories into an anthology to be published by Blackwood's, was continuing to write *The Birthday*, and embarking on her most ambitious prose work, a collection of essays and short stories. These included *The Grave of the Broken Heart*, and *Andrew Cleves*, two of her best tragic pieces, as well as a light-hearted satirical look at morning worshippers at Boldre church, stratified in their social positions. The *Chapters* were being published in Blackwood's magazine and were later to appear in two volumes.

Meanwhile, her beloved old nurse who had come from Jersey with her grandmother, had fallen ill, and Caroline nursed her faithfully, much of *Andrew Cleves* being written by her bedside, where she also continued to struggle with her portion of *Robin Hood*, because however difficult the metre, this was her chief link in her lifeline to Robert.

"I have returned to my old habit of writing before breakfast," Robert wrote. "Even at this rate a long poem may be completed in two months - and that if I hold on, providing you bear your part and keep pace with me, half that time will complete our purpose and we shall build something more durable if not more beautiful than the best castle either of us has ever erected, architects though we have both been. Now dear Caroline, go you to work in the same mind."

This is very revealing of Robert's attitude to his work - so much to be got done in such a time. Force of circumstances had made him write to tailored length - whatever editors wanted, since the family must be fed and Greta Hall maintained.

Caroline struggled on with *Robin Hood*, but still found herself unable to master the metre and thus enjoy writing it. Perhaps she was inhibited by her own lack of confidence - every line had to be as good as Robert's.

"I send you what will I think be my first and last contribution to the grand coalition, for you cannot fail to perceive from this specimen how utterly incapable I am of fulfilling your expectations ... it is mortifying to find myself excluded by my own inadequacy from so delightful an association. I tried to begin the second canto; but enough of this nonsense. Do not you relinquish the plan."

So *Robin Hood* had to be laid aside, to be taken up by them both at a much later date. Further on in the same letter she tells Robert of her latest illness.

"I have been very seriously ill almost ever since I last wrote; very ill in body, worse in mind, in my head; sometimes in that state, that if I had had a friend near me, I should have caught hold of him, imploring him to save me from - I know not what. I was getting a little better when your last letter arrived. The wind came to the south that day, and I was allowed to breathe it in the gravel walk before the house, when a bee came humming about me with its summer sound. These three circumstances did me the world of good - your letter most - far most, and then in a fit of grateful valour, I set about my task. I had put it off and off till then from a cowardly misgiving, and lo! you have the result. Pray do not love me the less because I have thus disappointed your expectations."

In this last sentence she uses the word love, perhaps jokingly on the page, but certainly in all truth in her heart. Why did she not abandon this tiresome metrical corset and revert to the freedom of blank verse for her own part of *Robin Hood* - it seems thoughtless of Robert not to suggest this, when the collaboration obviously meant so much to her.

"Pray write to me, if only to scold," she finishes. "What would I give for only one poor half hour of your society now and then." Robert replied to this really heart-breaking letter with a concise essay on metre, and all about heroic cadences, but he did say, "I wish I were with you," even if it were to give her a lesson in prosody! Robert had projected *Robin Hood* in the first place as a personal link, but also to form a respectable partnership the world could acknowledge and which might be acceptable to his family. Though he had always been a traveller, Edith being used to his frequent absences and visits to friends, his staying with a single woman in her southern cottage must have seemed *odd*, if nothing more. Now, as part of his profession, it could be accounted for. He was to pay more visits, but *Robin Hood* was to be the excuse rather than the reason. In spite of his happy marriage, Robert was obviously deeply fond of Caroline by now, entering into all her interests and daily life with his warm concern.

One of his poems shows this concern. He was at this time busy writing *Oliver Newman*, and *The Tale of Paraguay*, his interest in South

America being an offshoot of his earlier visits to Portugal, but he found time, at Caroline's request to write an elegy for her cousin Paul Burrard, the son of Uncle Harry, who had been killed in the Peninsular War. Robert's poem was later published as one of a series of *Inscriptions*.

> For gallant as he was, and blithe of heart
> Expert of hand and keen of eye and prompt
> In intellect, religion was the crown
> Of all his noble properties.

This may not be great poetry, but it brought real comfort to Caroline's much loved aunt, Hannah Burrard.

1824 was not a good year, all round. Robert was ill for much of the early summer and Caroline's old nurse, the last of that loving circle which had enwrapped her childhood, died at last, leaving Caroline physically exhausted after months of nursing and emotionally at her lowest ebb.

"My present state is a very restless one," she wrote to Robert at the end of August. "I am suffering terribly, night and day, from past over excitement and the dead calm that has succeeded to it ... The next sixth of December [her birthday] will be doubly a wintry day to me, for it will be the first in my remembrance that will bring with it no tribute of affection. My dear *bonne*, according to the custom of her country, used always to bring me a nosegay on that morning; yes, flowers even on that wintry day; and I believe if we had dwelt on the Great St Bernard she would have contrived to find some among the eternal snows. No voice, no kiss, no flowers now. It will all be winter." There was no thought of a visit to Keswick that summer. So Robert did his best to cheer her spirits through autumn and winter, sending further instalments of *Robin Hood*, and letters full of warm sympathy. "Sick and alone are sad words in themselves and more so when they are coupled. If wishes could avail you should be well, and here."

During the winter she sent a little sketch of herself, for which Robert hastens to say, "You have sent me one of the things in the world which I most wished to possess ... You are lonely, God knows; yet, if you could know how much I was with you in thought, you would feel that there is one person in the world who regards you as you ought to be regarded - as you would wish him to regard you. How difficult it is when we mean a great deal, not to say either too little or too much."

What really dragged Caroline from her slough of despond was the prospect of a spring visit from Robert. She did confess that after her mother's death, she had longed to die. "I seem to have stepped over a great gulf dividing me from my early years and from my early friends. My wish would have been, I think, not to overstep it, not to have gone farther." But she goes on to say, "But you met and took me by the hand on the brink of that dreary, unknown country: I found in you what I never met with, even in my lost Eden, and while you hold me fast I shall not want courage to go on, nor inclination to tarry yet a little longer, should it be God's pleasure.

At present I am disposed to be very much in love with life and very unwilling to leave it before May. I had no idea whatever of moving from home at that time, and I would not for the world receive your visit anywhere else, because your having been here, (even for that visit volant you must prepare me to expect) will leave a brightness over many succeeding months, and I, as well as you, converse with shadows. If it were good and pleasant for you to stay some length of time here, how hard I would try to keep you! But what is best for yourself, that shall be best for me, so come without fear of persecution."

It *was* only a flying visit. Caroline had originally been assigned the women, children and forest background in their poem of *Robin Hood*. When Robert arrived at Buckland full of warmth and enthusiasm, she was glad he had ignored her previous refusal to write more of their joint work. In fact she had written her part and even added some verses, which "found favour beyond its deserts."

They also made plans for another visit when Robert returned from a summer visit to Europe, but this was not to be, as he injured a foot while abroad and found it necessary on landing to make straight for his doctor brother in Harley Street.

Caroline was collecting some of her miscellaneous pieces into an anthology. Asked to name it, Robert suggested *A Woman's Portfolio, Autumnal Flowers*, and *Solitary Hours*, the one chosen. In her correspondence with William Blackwood, the mysterious Captain Bruce appears again. He would seem to have been on a visit to Scotland where he was entertained by Walter Scott at Abbotsford, where he also met William Blackwood. Robert's foot was still troubling him, so he was unable to meet William Canning, the politician, at Storrs, as planned. "Unexpectedly Sir Walter Scott made his appearance there, and came from thence to see me," Robert wrote. "We had not met for twelve years and I found him greatly changed, grown large, perfectly grey, and with the look of three score which is about five years older than he is."

Caroline wrote to William Blackwood, "Captain Bruce told me he had made interest with Mr Blackwood for a few autobiographical scraps [meaning hand written] - especially of Sir Walter Scott's writing. If Mr B would forward a few when he has opportunity - the impudence of collectors is notorious. Captain Bruce, newly landed in Calcutta, wished to be remembered."

One of the younger Blackwoods was to learn the printing trade from the bottom, starting with the ink used. Caroline had written to Captain Bruce hoping he might befriend the young man, which he did, writing to her, "I am very glad to know young Blackwood - he is a very fine young man. I shall be happy to be of service to him. I have no doubt he will do well in the indigo factory." Later he asked young Blackwood to dinner. One longs to hear more of this kindly person. He had a son of school age, so presumably a wife, but Caroline never mentions her, only writing this further enigmatic paragraph in a later letter to William Blackwood,

Caroline Bowles

Robert Southey

Buckland Cottage 1997

GRETA HALL AND KESWICK BRIDGE.

thus adding to the Indian mystery. "A son of Captain Bruce's and a little Persian boy of whom I have charge are going out this month on the Roxburgh Castle. If you should like to send to your son at Calcutta, it might be entrusted to these youths."

Who is the Persian boy? Does she mean that both boys were entrusted to her care? They are not mentioned ever to Robert. Possibly they were at boarding school and spent their holidays at Buckland.

Caroline's correspondence with Blackwood's reveals a quite different side of her character. She is not at all afraid to stand firm over what she wants published and in what manner, sending a very stiff note at the delay in printing *Solitary Hours*, though often behindhand with her own contributions for which she pleads ill health. When one of the *Chapters on Churchyards* appeared in the magazine with some typographical errors, she wrote, "Pray Mr Blackwood, cuff me the compositor who set my last chapter. He has made me write nonsense and vile grammar."

Mr Blackwood is an indulgent publisher, writing personal queries after her health, giving her a retaining fee and sending parcels of books at frequent intervals, which included Mrs Heman's *Poems*, De Quincey and Walter Scott.

Robert meanwhile was positively wallowing in books as he loved to do. "My books [bought on his European travels] arrived a fortnight ago. And I was as happy as the arrival of eighty nine folios and about as many smaller fry could make me. The honeymoon is not over yet. O dear Caroline, what a blessing it is to have an insatiable appetite of this kind, which grows by what it feeds on. The only thing I wish for now and then, is the presence of someone who could fairly enter into my views and feelings and partake the interest which I take in such researches."

By this time Caroline had had her sketch of their largest Lakeland picnic lithographed, and sent Robert a copy. Though he makes the best of it, obviously the younger ones had mocked at it. Kate seemed not to have taken to Caroline even then; this indifference was to grow to bitter hatred years later.

"Two days ago I had a very pleasant surprise in unrolling the lithograph of our party on Honister Crag. It is a very pleasant memorial, and likely to be valued one of these days for your sake and for mine, when we shall be far off on our celestial journey, travelling, I hope, together. Will it not be delightful to visit the man in the moon, go from thence to the evening star with a wish and make a trip to the sun as familiarly as now we might to the sea, and put ourselves upon a comet, instead of getting into a stage coach!

Miss Fryer's likeness is very well preserved and Dame Elizabeth also may be recognised by those who know her, John Calvert's back too is a good likeness, but the lithographer has uglified all the rest and Kate and Belle dispute for which of them the ugliest of the imps is intended. But it is happily caught and managed and like everything that I see of yours, makes me wish more and more that we were near enough to set each other to work, and to work in unison."

Caroline did not often use her pen to raise a smile: when she does, one wishes she had chosen the light satirical vein more often. Her next letter looks forward to his promised visit in May, but also sketches the latest craze in Lymington, religious societies. "All womankind is whirling round in a vortex of religious dissipation - and their energies once set going pass my comprehension. Go where one will, the subject is forced upon one. One lady's drawing-room is full of little charity boxes, placed here and there among the ornamental litter; another keeps a stall of trumpery knick-knacks-ladies' work to lay her visitors under contribution; another asks you to work for her (audacious!) and then a whole bevy of damsels sit congregated together, pasting and painting, and sewing and gilding, and what not, to get up a booth for the next religious fair," which much amused Robert. But she finishes, "If I had wings like a dove ... they should bear me today to some of your haunts, among the windings of Greta or the mountain dells, where methinks there must be healing in the grey air, and music, I am sure, in the voice of a friend."

Once again, the spring visit could only be a short one. Robert and Caroline walked in the New Forest where beech and oak were in their first brilliant green, bird song was at its height and the free-ranging ponies watched over their leggy, new-born foals. They took a trip to Southampton on the Hythe ferry, for the rest Robert had to keep up with his reviews, and they worked together on *Robin Hood*, though Caroline still found the metre difficult.

As soon as he had gone, to his brother, Henry, in London, *en route* for Europe, Caroline must needs write, "God bless you for coming to see me. The words were in my heart, and on my lips when I parted with you, though they found no utterance, so my pen must convey them to you. I feel by what sacrifice of time and convenience you have given me the highest gratification which could possibly fall to my lot, but I know at the same time you will never reckon as lost time days you devoted to that charitable purpose."

To which Robert speedily replied, "Dear Caroline, God bless you. You have no reason to thank me for a visit, from which, short as it necessarily was, and therefore in part painful, I derived as much pleasure as it is possible that I could give."

He returned to England a month later with a chest full of books and in excellent spirits. "But I am going home, to be at rest I trust, and get my after dinner sleep and to be cool - and to be clean - and to write prose and also to write verse, and go on the lake, and play with the cats and talk nonsense with the children, and learn Dutch with Cuthbert and receive proof sheets, and rub through life as smoothly and pleasantly as I can." This is a splendid summary of Robert's daily life, hard work and his loved ones and fun all mixed together and totally excluding Caroline. Then he adds the one sentence that could make all the difference. "If I could have you within sight I would not ask Fortune for much more."

But Fortune had a terrible blow in store for Robert. At Greta Hall he found thirteen year old Belle seriously ill: two weeks after he wrote that happy letter from Harley Street, Belle died. To his wife Edith this was a blow from which she was never fully to recover. Depression and ill health were to grow only worse as the years passed. Caroline did the only thing possible for her, wrote a poem. Sadly, it is by no means one of her best.

> Tis ever thus - tis ever thus when Hope hath built a bower
> Like that of Eden, wreathed about with every thornless flower
> To dwell therein securely the self deceiver's trust.
> A whirlwind from the desert comes, and all is in the dust.

Every verse begins with the same six words, which seem to devalue what follows into an everyday occurrence. The poem is totally impersonal, with no direct reference to the real Belle, who, after all, she had met, and would strike any readers of Wordsworth or Coleridge as very old-fashioned in style. Perhaps she was not that pleased with it herself, for she did not send it to Robert. Later he was to come upon it by accident in a magazine where it was simply entitled *On the Death of a Young Lady*. He read it to Edith and wrote to the author, "She expressed that sort of pleasure which deep grief is capable of feeling. Thank you dear friend, thank you, thank you." So at least it served a purpose.

Originally Robert had invited Caroline to come and stay for the whole of the following summer: now he must devote himself to his own family, particularly Edith, whom he decided to take to Harrogate for a change of scene, and the drinking of the waters at this fashionable spa. Caroline tried staunchly to hide her own bitter disappointment. "I am glad you are to move early in May, and can well understand the comfort it will be to have all your dear ones with you. I know your horror of locomotion but truly I cannot fancy you a watering place visitor, a pump room lounger. I should as soon expect to meet an eagle sauntering up Bond Street. I would, if I could do what I liked - betake myself to Harrogate, in the hope of being noticed by you and your family" But this was not to be. One wonders why she did not in fact visit the spa, since she had reserved the summer for Keswick - perhaps because Robert had not suggested it.

Harrogate society was, as Caroline knew, hardly to Robert's taste. When he and the family returned to Greta Hall in July, he wrote, "Here we are, Edith and Bertha the better for the Harrogate waters, their mother only better inasmuch as the new circumstances there may sometimes serve to withdraw her from the melancholy and hopeless course of her habitual thoughts and feelings - a sore grief, of which I never before said as much as is now expressed here to any human being, but which presses upon me more heavily than my bodily infirmities."

This short paragraph reveals a new situation - Robert confiding in Caroline about his wife, a circumstance common to mistresses but hardly to literary friends. Whether Caroline recognised that their friendship had assumed a new dimension it is difficult to tell, for she replies in such mannered prose. "Well I know there are griefs far heavier to be borne than any bodily infirmity. If human sympathy could lighten yours, how greatly would the weight be lessened! The perpetual sight of constitutional despondency in one nearly and dearly connected with us is an eating sorrow - one that began to prey upon me from my earliest recollection - and has no doubt cast its shadow over a temper naturally joyous."

Here she is referring back to her father's nervous state. One cannot help wishing that she could have replied with more natural warmth.

She does continue her letter though with a cheerful little story about a visit from William Lisle Bowles, the vicar-poet of Bremhill who claimed to be her cousin. He was looking well and seemed in remarkably cheerful spirits, anxious to tell her a strange story that Lady Beaumont had heard, how much Caroline adored Wordsworth, felt sure she and Caroline were kindred spirits and proposed to write, asking her to come and live in her house. Mr Bowles had done his utmost to dissuade her from such a plan. "Admire and delight in Mr Wordsworth's noble poetry I certainly do. 'Adore' Mr Wordsworth I certainly do not," Caroline wrote. "You know you could hardly send me to see Mr Wordsworth even with your passport. This effusion of dignified indignation will amuse you I think; but perhaps you are not surprised to learn that I can be a little bit of a virago."

Lady Beaumont was known as a woman of great warmth and charm, fond of espousing good causes and writers in need. She and her husband, Sir George, had long ago befriended Coleridge and Wordsworth and were well known to Robert. Incidentally this letter finally refutes the story of Wordsworth taking Caroline round the Lakes on a pony, declaiming his poems the while, on her visit to Keswick.

Robert however can see some practical value in at least a friendship with Lady Beaumont. "I wish you knew her, and should be very glad if she invited you to visit, and carried you from London to Coleortan. You would then be in reasonable reach of Keswick, and I would call for you there on my next return from the south." (The Beaumont's Coleorton estate was in Leicestershire) But Caroline did not pursue this plan. Robert too was making an effort to be cheerful and gives her a colourful description of a large family bonfire party with the Wordsworths on the shore of Leatheswater, twenty eight of them. "There comes Burn'em wood," said Mr Barber as Willie Wordsworth was bringing a huge load of sticks for the fire; upon which Mr Quillinan (Dora Wordsworth's husband) rejoined, "You shall not be called dunce inane for saying that."

By the autumn of that year Robert was already making plans for the following spring. He would visit his brother in Harley Street in May, then take one of the new steam coaches which would whisk him to Southampton in no time, *en route* to visit her. "But I will make it my last movement if you will muster heart and hope to travel northwards, under my care, and pass the remainder of the summer and autumn with us. Can you? Will you? Nothing is more likely to do you good than this mountain air."

chapter six

The lion's tail

Robert came at midsummer and Caroline kept most visitors at bay, so that he could enjoy perfect quiet in Buckland Cottage, secluded behind its tall trees. Only once, for one of her family did Caroline open the door, so that the Poet Laureate of England might be glimpsed at work. "When you had shown my mane and tail," exclaimed her guest, "you might as well have let me roar." Robert was working on a long poem, *The Pilgrimage to Compostella*. They walked in the large, rambling garden where Caroline read to him the beginning of her poem, *Santarem*, Robert having a double interest in this work as he had sent her the story and now, as always, was encouraging her to finish it.

But they did not work all the time. There were walks in the forest with Caroline perched on her Shetland pony, Robert striding at her side with the dogs, the woods at the height of their beauty, with glades full of tall foxgloves, young foals taking their first gallops, fallow deer in their elegant summer coats of dappled chestnut with leggy fawns hidden in the newly unfolded bracken. They also went bathing, probably at Milford on Sea, two miles to the west, for the coast around Lymington itself was a wild stretch of marshland and dikes interrupted here and there by salt pans. With all the fresh air, the peace of the quiet cottage, and Caroline's companionship, the insomnia which had been troubling Robert dropped away. In long discussions of books, in sharing his writing plans with Caroline and listening to hers, all the worries that had beset him at Greta Hall disappeared - for a little while. It was a time of gentle happiness for them both.

But there was no more talk of her returning with him to Keswick for the rest of the summer. Was this because of Caroline's health, always fragile, or her sense of delicacy? Did she feel unable to stay in Edith Southey's house when she was bound to Robert with such ties of affection?

The following year Robert did not visit at all. He wrote of a rumour that he was to be offered some post at King's College, London. "I should neither be inclined nor qualified . . . yet when this letter put the possiblity into my head, I had waking dreams half the night of how easy a distance it would be from London to Buckland, and were the matter ever seriously to be weighed, that consideration would be one of the weightiest in the scale. I would give a great deal to be near you." While Edith was alive, that was the nearest Robert could come to a declaration of love.

In 1829 he did not visit either, but sent her an extraordinarily generous and loving gift - the dedication of his new book of poems containing *All for Love*, and *The Pilgrimage to Compostella*.

TO CAROLINE BOWLES

> Could I look forward to a distant day
> With hope of building some elaborate lay,
> Then would I wait till worthier strains of mine
> Might bear inscribed thy name, O Caroline;
> For I would, while my voice is heard on earth,
> Bear witness to thy genius and thy worth.

Did he really think that Caroline's talent for poetry amounted to genius? Caroline was altogether overcome.

First of all she felt surprised, then deeply unworthy of such an honour and indeed prayed to become more worthy, with a gush of tears.

Gratitude made her try to set pen to paper, but she was too moved to write straight away, and still weak from an attack of sickness. Finally she did write in affectionate gratitude and feeling much better. "I do not care to die while you remain to me, though I should like just to take precedence" - a wish not to be granted.

Robert's dedicatory poem, which all the world might read, seems really to have lifted her spirits, also it was springtime, and like many depressed people, Caroline was more than ordinarily affected by the weather. Her May letter is unusually light-hearted.

"Yesterday and today, almost our first spring days, have revived me so far as to enable me to get down into the lower flower garden, lured thither by the attraction of a new plaything which was sent to me two days ago - would Cuthbert could see it! - a little horse, just three feet high, a perfect little creature, mouse-coloured, with black mane, tail and feet, and following me like a dog about the garden and on into the house, where the first interview between him and Mufti [the dog] was delightful, both eating bread together at the same time out of my hand, with their noses touching. When you were last in fairyland, did you hear the name of Titania's palfrey? If you did, pray let me know it that mine may be so christened, and then he shall have green housings with silver bells. Oh if he were of the true elfin breed, how soon he should set me down at the door of Greta Hall."

It is more than two months since Robert sent his poems, but her mind is still full of the dedication. She ends, "Fare you well dear friend, I leave you for your Colloquies. I think my name looks beautiful in print. I never liked it so well before."

There is also news of her mysterious adopted boy - it is tempting to guess that he is the son of Captain Bruce, since he first wrote to her from Bushire in Persia and had lately spoken of returning there to look for a house. "My little Persian charge, now in his sixteenth year, though not looking eleven, is going out at the end of the month in the Roxburgh

Castle, and I send him up to London in about ten days time to be fitted out. He has turned out most happily; but I am fearful the poor fellow is now taken away very prematurely from his school, to be placed in a mercantile house at Calcutta."

All this time she had been writing the separate stories of *Chapters on Churchyards* which had been appearing in Blackwood's Magazine: now they were published in two volumes, her most substantial prose work, which was to be reprinted many times both in Britain and America.

It is an uneven collection, like most anthologies of magazine pieces, the later ones of far greater depth, though the earlier stories do reveal Caroline's often hidden sense of humour. Chapter one, for example, tells how she came upon the year old grave of the local Squire, which his distraught widow had planted with lilac and honeysuckle, being grazed over by the parson's house cow. When she begins a moral homily to the boy herding it, he interrupts her, "Ees, Squire been dead twelve month last Whitsuntide, 'an thick be his'n monument an' madam was married last week to our Measter an' thick be our cow." Why not plant annuals, she suggests, to new widows.

In similar vein, here is Madam Buckwheat's grave, from Chapter four. "Here stands a fine tall freestone, ornamented in basso-relievo, with a squat white urn swaddled up in ponderous drapery, over which droops a gilt weeping willow - it looks like a sprig of samphire - the whole set off by a blue ground, encircled by a pair of goosewings - oh no, I cry the sculptor's mercy, they are the pinions of a cherubim."

Chapter five is an account of simple Rachel Maythorne, seduced by a farm worker at gleaning time, interesting for her account of the girl's funeral. "The pall is borne by six girls each shrouded like a nun in her long white hood and in lieu of the black pall, a white sheet flung over the coffin." This recalls the funeral of Caroline's cousin, Laura Burrard, who was found dead on the eve of her wedding: a similar procession, though of course larger, made its way from Walhampton across the river to Lymington churchyard.

The next three chapters are all about the village, church and manor of 'Haliburn' - not really stories with a plot, but descriptive pieces delightful in their detail. This is the Housekeeper's room. "A fine old-fashioned place with huge gaping fireplace; deep narrow windows in thick walls, old oak benches and tables with voluted legs, ranges of bright pewter and fine old Delf - huge round dishes with scalloped edges - antique tea kettles - spits on which an ox might have been roasted whole - coffee pots and chocolate pots and posset pots and porringers and pipkins, little squat things upon three feet that looked as if they could toddle about by themselves and vessels and utensils of all shapes and sizes, wares and metals whose proper use it would have puzzled any soul to determine."

Chapters nine, ten and eleven are similar in style, describing a visit to the Somerset village of 'Broad Summerford'. O.E. in her article, claims that this was the farm where Caroline stayed during her visit to Jersey, but this seems unlikely since nothing in it rings false to Somerset. Again, there is little plot, but much gently humorous description. For a party, "There began such compounding of seed cakes and pound cakes and plain cakes and wafers and crumpets and all sorts of indescribable accompaniments such as might have set up a dozen confectioners' shops. And then there was such a stuffing of turkey poults - such larding of capons - such collaring of eels, such potting of savoury meats, such whipping of syllabubs, such spinning of sugar - such powdering with comfits - such devices and surprises, almond hedgehogs and floating islands included."

But it is in the last long stories - and they *are* stories in the true sense, closely plotted with vivid characterisation - where Caroline shows her true powers of imagination. It is a great compliment to say they remind one of Thomas Hardy, since he was not yet born. Edward Dowden in his introduction to the letters of Robert and Caroline, says, "The sketches of English country life in these chapters are both bright and tender; and one tale, of conspicuously higher merit than the rest, *Andrew Cleves*, exhibits genuine tragic power."

Andrew is a hard, mean, respectable farmer, doting on his only child, Joe who gets in with bad company. Andrew mortgages the farm to pay off his son's debts, but all in vain. The youth is eventually hanged and Andrew takes the body home for burial.

Another, less dramatic, is *The Grave of the Broken Heart.* Genteel but poverty-stricken Millicent moves to Seavale and is soon engaged to the local curate, Horace Vernon. They wait four years for him to be offered a proper living; meanwhile Lady Octavia comes to stay at the Vicarage, "a very lovely, gay, good humoured, captivating creature of nineteen, brilliantly accomplished and (as everybody said) with the best heart in the world." This is Lady Octavia passing Millicent's home. "What a sweet cottage - and there's the person who sat in the next pew to my uncle's at church this morning, looking so wretchedly forlorn and sickly, but really genteel for that sort of person, and must have been rather pretty when she was young, poor thing . . . I quite adore the cottage - it's so like our poultry woman's." Horace calls on Millicent less often. When etiquette forces her to call at the vicarage, Lady Octavia trills, "I'm sure I'm quite shocked, Miss Aboyne," with the sweetest, deprecating manner in the world, "at monopolising so much of Mr Vernon's time, but he is so kind and obliging; when he is once comfortably established on that ottoman," pointing to one at the foot of her harp, "there's no driving him away, though I often tell him." - even Millicent's gentle spirit was moved by the obvious malice and impertinence and she made her farewell curtsey. Given the title the rest may be surmised.

There is an extraordinary difference in depth and accomplishment between the early and late *Chapters on Churchyards*. Perhaps Caroline was gaining in confidence all the time. Also it seems that her imagination did not really flow until she was writing entirely from it, rather than using remembered anecdotes from the past.

As ever, Robert was encouraging over her *Chapters*, but wished she would use her undoubted sense of humour more often, rather than add to readers' sorrows with such stories as these.

She continued in good spirits with the spring, delighting in Oberon, the new pony, and her dog Mufti. "Tell Cuthbert my dog is quite big enough for him to ride, measures two yards and a quarter from the tip of his nose to the end of his tail, and every now and then walks away by mistake with the tea table upon his back. He is like a great white lion curled all over, with black nose and ears."

By July she felt confident and well enough to suggest to Robert that they might bring out a joint book of separate poems, since she had despaired of mastering the metre demanded by *Robin Hood* and their working together any further on it. Robert wrote back at once, "I will rather send a few lines, dear Caroline, than let a post go by without telling you that the wish which you have expressed has been more than once on the top of my pen, and would have very soon found its way to paper. I should dearly like it in effect. So go you to work. Moreover, please you not consider the original scheme [*Robin Hood*] as abandoned, but only as in abeyance, till you will let me bring you to pass a summer and autumn here."

She did not go to Greta Hall with its wide airy views of mountain and lake, but stayed at home and complained of the weather, "Oh for a little summer. I long for it as for life; so reviving is it to me to bask in the sun and live in the open air. For the first time in my life I have quarrelled with trees, green trees, for being shut in weeks together by the perpetual floods and storms. The perpetual mopping and mowing of an old acacia, top heavy with rain, has so worried me by day, and haunted me by night, that I could fancy it my evil genius."

But she was writing still. Whether in reaction to the tragic themes of *Chapters in Churchyards*, or because Robert had several times taunted her with being a cruel writer to make her readers dwell on such misery, she began a little comic squib, for Cuthbert, *The Cat's Tail, being the history of Childe Merlin,* by the Baroness de Katzleben - one more instance of her life revolving round the Southeys, but there is good news of her own family the following year. "Some near relations of mine who formerly lived in the neighbourhood and are now returning to end their days here, a Mr and Mrs Rooke. She lived much in my father's house before she married, has always been in kindness and affection a second mother to me, and the person of all others in my own family on whom I rely most in time of need."

Now that Robert can picture the Buckland background to her life, her letters become more natural, and are often full of delightful little homely stories. "I have three nightingales in my little flower garden; that I not only hear, but see them sing, so fearlessly do they sit in the boughs of an acacia over my head (one of them at least, and his rivals hard by on neighbouring trees) Last winter, during that long sharp frost, one of my blackbirds got so desperate from starvation, that he actually hopped into Mufti's house in the backyard, and disputed his bones with him. Mufti's astonishment overcame his indignation and Blacky hopped off with such a bone as I could not have believed his beak could have lifted. I heard the cuckoo this morning for the first time."

Unfortunately *The Cat's Tail* proved difficult to publish, so in the end she revealed all to Robert. "I got up the story of my cat in sublime style - a feline epic - illustrated with appropriate pen etchings, wrote a very solemn preface and pleased myself all the while with the thought of the said epic's presenting itself at Keswick, all unannounced. Then I had been told that your great man, the Hybrid, [Robert's publisher, Murray] was the most likely gudgeon in the world to bite at any hook baited with rank and fashion and half my sport was the idea of getting him to bring out my nonsense. So, I took a foreign title, sealed with a foreign coat of arms, all coronet, and sent my mss. in a dashing carriage, to match, through the hand of a fair friend who was charmed to manage the intrigue and whose air of fashion must add its weight. But she could not see Murray and left the mss. At the end of a fortnight he returned it with a civil note. I tried two other printers with no other success, so I lost my little joke." Robert said he would have known who had written it, whoever published it.

The Cat's Tail was eventually published the following year by Blackwood, under the Baroness alias, Caroline sketching three illustrations for it, which were etched by Cruikshank.

But she did look to far wider horizons than are suggested by the cat book. Speaking French like a native she had been much involved with the French who had fled to Lymington in her teenage years and one of her childhood playmates had been the Princess de Polignac whose father had been away, at first fighting, then a prisoner of Napoleon. So now Caroline was taking a keen interest in the turbulent events in France, where, six years before, Charles X had been proclaimed king and had later set up a government with his favourite, Jules de Polignac at its head. But this had just been defeated and once more there were riots in Paris, against the restoration of the nobility, the power of the church and the poverty in the streets. Charles abdicated in favour of his grandson, and made the Duke of Orleans, Governor General of France - though the people wanted him as king. Gathering up his family and remnants of the court, Charles made his way to Cherbourg, a puzzled, child-like figure in his seventies. Remembering the fate of the last French king caught up in revolution, he prudently set sail for England, and once more the South Coast became a haven for the French nobility.

So it was with some excitement that Caroline wrote to Robert after an excursion on her little pony. "I am just returned from an evening ride and I believe I have met - whom do you think? - travelling along our Hampshire road, in a brizka and four, without a single attendant or outrider - no less personages, I verily believe than the ex-king of France and Madame Duchesse d'Angouleme, on their road to Lulworth Castle, lent them by my neighbours and acquaintances the Welds, who have preceded the royal exiles to prepare for their reception. I suspect the rest of the party have proceeded by water, but am almost sure the King and Duchess (whom I knew formally) were those who passed me. What a dream of greatness! What an abrupt transition! The ladies of the party have been living at the Fountain Inn at Cowes, for many days, walking about on the pier there and at Ryde and talking to everybody who seemed inclined to talk to them. It was signified to the King and Dauphin, who also wished to land, that it might be unsafe, so great is the spirit of exasperation against them; so they remained on board, the King, gazing at the crowds assembled by a regatta, and greatly increased by the curiosity to see him and his family. This place has actually been depopulated, such is the rush towards Cowes of every creature that could move - except me, who would fain have been further than I am even here from a sight so painful."

Robert too was worried by the events in France. Soon however it is the troubled state of England itself which invades the correspondence. Robert had business in London in November and intended to journey on to Caroline, afterwards visiting the West Country. "My dear friend," she wrote in November, "I am so panic-stricken at the aspect of the times, that I feel as if I longed to draw everyone I love close round me, that the same fate at least may involve us; but perhaps those who listen in darkness and loneliness to the advancing tide may be apt to fancy it approaches more awfully and impetuously than it does in reality."

The tide was a desperate need for reform. There were more agricultural riots in Hampshire and Dorset the previous month against the price of corn, the new machines and the terrible divide between rural poverty and the Lords who sat in parliament - evidenced by the punishments laid down by the court in Salisbury. No blood had been shed by the mobs, only property damaged and ricks burned, but thirty four men were sentenced to death and almost four hundred transported to Australia. Meanwhile the new industrial cities such as Manchester had no members of parliament, though the tiny hamlet of Newtown, in the Isle of Wight had two. The new Radical party campaigned ceaselessly for this ridiculous state of affairs to be brought to an end and were incensed when the Duke of Wellington, the Prime Minister, addressing the new session of parliament in November, said he could see no reason for altering the present system of representation. This caused uproar all over the country, especially in the industrial towns where some workers decided to march on London. By this time, Robert was in the capital, where law and order was now in the hands of the new police force, set up by Robert Peel the previous year. More interested than frightened, Robert sent a dispatch of the news.

"I do not wonder, dear friend, that the state of affairs should appear more formidable to you at a distance than it does to me upon the spot. I believe that the intention was to murder the king, as well as the Duke, and to set London on fire, and I know there was a plan for massacreing the new policemen. The streets on Monday and Tuesday were crowded with a set of dirty, resolute looking men, evidently collected for some purpose, a great part of them not being Londoners, but from Manchester and other such hot beds of mischief. I should have been struck by their appearance and their extraordinary numbers, even if I had not had to make my way among them with a cheque for a hundred pounds in my pocket into Coutt's bank and to come out of it with the bills. However, I brought them safely home, and slept very soundly, though the last thing which I saw was a strong body of police drawn up under the front windows."

He goes on to tell her good humouredly that he is hungry, only having consumed a dozen oysters that day and is looking forward to dinner with his publisher, Murray, ending, "You see that I have neither lost my spirits nor my appetite. No man sees the danger more clearly in its whole extent, and no one, I believe, fears it less. My trust is in God's mercy, and my stand upon the rock of ages. Farewell dear Caroline. I shall be glad to find myself on the road to Hampshire."

It does seem strange that Robert, who had once planned a Utopia of equals on the banks of the Sussquehanna, should side with the establishment now, against reform. Even his deeply held Christian faith did not extend much charity to the radicals who were trying to improve the labourer's lot: neither did Caroline's.

Within a fortnight, Lymington itself had become the scene of violence and though Caroline lived for Robert's visits, she feared for his safety. "If the present state of affairs goes on, dear friend, your intended visit to me must be relinquished, or you will pay it at some peril to yourself.. We have as yet had no fires nearer than Southampton. But many threatening letters are received - night watches are established, and a most extraordinary measure resorted to here - all the smugglers with their chief captain of this coast called in and organised to act in our defence with the Preventive Servicemen! Then the male population is converted, as in other places, into special constables - two thirds of them on condition that they shall not be obliged to act unless - what do you think? - they like it! and I have not the slightest doubt that six old women might rout the whole posse with their bodkins and knitting needles. At a meeting of magistrates, gentlemen and farmers, assembled the other day in the Town Hall, the sight of a pitiful village mob marching towards them frightened them so heartily that some poked their heads out of the window to promise everything, before anything was asked ...

The ringleader of that band of mobbers was so kind as to stop at my door on his triumphant way back and volunteer a detail of their successes, not forgetting to dwell with great compassion on having 'frightened the poor gentlemen terribly'. I should not feel much apprehension were it not for the travelling mob of nearly two thousand, perambulating the county, actually sacking and plundering houses. The carriages coming here today from Fordingbridge describe that place as having the appearance of having been sacked and pillaged - which in fact it had been in great degree. The Cootes of Westcourt, near Fordingbridge, defended their house gallantly with only six men, drove off the rioters, but poor young Coote was badly wounded. An express came in yesterday for help for Lord Cavan of Fawley, eleven miles from hence. How he fared I know not... but the vagrant mob, really a fearful one was at Hythe yesterday, nearly two thousand strong, - twelve miles from here. I had felt very safe from our mob, from my own insignificance, but have been the only individual in this neighbourhood who has had cause for serious apprehension - a threshing machine in a barn almost touching my premises, which the owners would not give up and the mob would have: and so for three days I have been receiving warnings from various quarters to get rid of my neighbour's, or it would be made into a bonfire with the premises it stood in, and mine could not escape, and I believe the attack was delayed for my sake. But at last the obstinate farmer gave up his machine, and it has been torn to pieces this morning - to my infinite joy.

One very odd thing I must tell you - all the dogs are turned radicals and ought to be reported to the government, Mufti not excepted. Every night and all night long now, every road and lane is perambulated by night watchers, they come into our premises, close to windows and doors, and not a dog, the most vigilant, restless and noisy, ever lifts up his voice at the disturbance in the faintest yelp or bark."

None of which put Robert off in the least and he arrived to spend Christmas with her. Once again they walked and wrote and talked together: for long hours Robert shut himself away working on *The New Colloquies*. His first book of Colloquies, in which he discussed topics of the hour, his library and the beauties of the Lake District with the ghost of Sir Thomas More, had been very well received. Now, working on the sequel, he would suddenly reappear with a sheaf of papers and straightway read them to Caroline so that they could discuss them immediately, something he could never do at home with Edith.

One of their excursions in the pony trap was to Burton, near Christchurch, a sentimental one for Robert, a seemingly odd choice. Probably Caroline expressed a wish to visit a place where he had once lived. For Burton was where he set up house in the happy, early days of his marriage to Edith. They had come down from London by stage-coach and driven through the woods in the full glory of spring. 'This New Forest is empty and lovely', he had written. 'I should like to have a house here and dispeople the rest, like the Conqueror.' At Burton they had entertained Robert's brother, Charles Lamb and Walter Scott in what Robert called his palace - two cottages made into one, with a view across a green valley, a shining river and a dark hill clothed with pines and a spacious garden complete with fishpond and a pigeon house.

When they came to visit this idyllic spot, Caroline noticed, with her quick sensitive eye for the feelings of others, that Robert's eyes were full of tears.

On January 4th 1831, Caroline wrote to William Blackwood, excusing her slowness in sending work by describing the disturbances round Lymington, and adding proudly, "My time became more agreeably engrossed by the society of Mr Southey who came to me about ten days ago and is still my inmate."

By the fire they discussed the wider issues of politics, and the French troubles, once again something he never did with Edith, for she had made the family and Greta Hall her whole world and since the death of Belle was liable to periods of deep depression, unable to take an interest even in her husband's affairs. Caroline devoted herself to his welfare, happy to have him in her house. She kept visitors at bay, showed him her neighbourhood, basked in his warmth.

As soon as he leaves for Bristol, she writes, to catch him there, "I am not yet reconciled to see the place opposite me vacant, and to feel only that you have been here. Writing to you steals me from myself a little while."

chapter seven

A perfect conformity of disposition

It would be a mistake to paint Caroline's life as a solitary one between Robert's visits. Her large family of Burrard and Rooke cousins, and various local friends included her in their social life when she was well enough and she was frequently called upon, as single women are, to help with sick or bereaved relatives. Her younger cousins, Laura and Frances sometimes came to stay. Also it seems likely that her kindly treatment by the rougher elements around Buckland was in gratitude for her own visits to their families in time of need. Lately she had been much at the Rooke house in Lymington where a cousin was seriously ill, but it was not all nursing, for later in the year, she went on a 'sea voyage,' as she describes it ecstatically, from Lymington right along the Solent to Portsmouth Harbour. There she spent three hours with Tom Rooke on board his ship, the Victory, no less, Sir Thomas Williams' flagship, even here thinking of Robert for his *Life of Nelson* was much in her mind.

She also enjoyed several literary friendships carried on largely by letter. One was with Mary Howitt, a prolific writer. Brought up a Quaker, she had married one William Howitt, an ardent liberal reformer of even stronger Quaker principles. They had settled in Nottingham, where William, working as a chemist, was soon to become an alderman of the city. He held strong opinions against the clergy and organised religion, which shocked Caroline's deep feeling for the church, so that she was constantly torn between an instinctive liking for Mary and a horror of her husband's views. Though Mary was some years younger than Caroline, they had much in common. Mary too had been educated at home and had started to write poetry when she was a young child: now she wrote mainly for children, except when collaborating with her husband. Some of her poems, such as *The Winter Fire* can still be found in anthologies of verse for children.

Robert wrote in May 1831. "You will be interested to hear that your friends the Howitts have taken Mrs Wordsworth into their house in a most helpless state, when she was completely laid up with an attack of sciatica at an inn. They had no personal acquaintance with the Wordsworths before, and there she is now and her daughter [Dora] with her."

Later he tells the sequel. "You ask about the Howitts. The Wordsworths left them full of gratitude for their kindness and full of liking for Mary. But her husband William, whom they might otherwise have liked much, had the reform fever upon him so strongly as to put the cloven foot of Quakerism offensively forward ... to poor Dora, who left the room when he had been exulting in the near downfall of the church - this to her when her brother and uncle are clergymen! He apologised after, having been well reproved for it by his wife."

After William brought out his *History of Priestcraft*, Caroline had thought it politic to drop the acquaintance, but receiving a letter and a book from Mary some time later, she told Robert this put her in a dilemma, since Mary was the only fellow authoress who had ever kept in touch with her. "I really 'took to her' as we say in Hampshire, but when I read some extracts from *Priestcraft* I shrank with horror at the thought of being the correspondent of the writer or his wife. But one day arrived her book, *The Seven Temptations of Man*, with a letter, such a gentle, charming, almost deprecating letter. She spoke of expecting the Wordsworths to stay with them on their way to London and expressed her hope and belief that I as well as the Wordsworths might still meet her and her husband on that neutral ground free only to subjects unconnected with politics and the party spirit. I could not turn from advances made in so kindly a spirit."

Robert also received Mary's book - she had hoped he might review it. Just as his life had embraced far wider horizons, both physically and emotionally than Caroline's, so his religious beliefs were less narrow than hers. Even so, his reaction to William Howitt shows the extraordinary hatred and resentment meted out to the dissenting faiths struggling for recognition in the nineteenth century. "I cannot review it, and have not yet found time to read it . . . It will be long before the animosities which have been so fiercely rekindled will subside. I am glad she has written to you. As for her husband, he is the very gall of bitterness, and the savour will abide upon him as long as he lives."

Caroline kept in touch with the Howitts though, and once mischievously suggested that Robert should meet William. "Mary has sent me another charming book she has just published for children, and he writes me a letter such as one can hardly fancy from the pen of the 'Nottingham Demagogue'. Shall I invite friend William to meet you here?" Perhaps this never came about, though later in the year both Howitts did visit Caroline - she found William good and kind though not one to mince words. To this news Robert replied darkly. "So you were pleased with the revolutionary Quaker. I should like to know how far he *is* a Quaker."

Caroline was by no means the only woman friend with whom Robert corresponded. He wrote humourous letters to Mary Barker who had been their neighbour in Keswick, and literary ones to various literary ladies including Mrs Hughes, Mrs Hodson and particularly to Anna Stothard Bray who was currently in the news. The wife of the vicar of Tavistock in Devon, she had discovered that her maid, Mary Colling, wrote poetry. A novelist herself and a woman of great kindness, Anna Bray collected funds and herself published Mary's poems, sending them to Robert for review. He relayed all this to Caroline as just the kind of story which would interest her, only to receive an uncharacteristically waspish reply.

How could Mrs Bray bear to have a maid so gifted - how would one treat her, she demanded. Was it in fact kind to encourage the poor girl above her station - who would she find to marry? All the old class conciousness instilled by grandmother-from-the-chateau comes leaping to the surface. One can only conclude that Caroline was actually jealous, not of so lowly a person as Mary Colling of course, but of Robert's interest in her and Anna Bray, who, in his usual encouraging way he had set to work collecting and retelling the legends of Devonshire. Caroline could not yet guess what part Anna was to play in her own life.

Other friends came and went in Caroline's life: she was particularly fond of the Levitt family who had recently given her a small new pony, called Pixie, but now they were moving right away from Lymington and her sadness at their going draws forth a heartfelt declaration of her feelings for her bedrock, Robert. "I turn impulsively to one whose correspondence only I would not exchange for personal intercourse with any human being, and who has led me by his hopeful spirit to look forward with more confidence and comfort than my weaker mind might have dared encourage to the renewal and perfecting in a better life of friendships contracted in holiness of heart, and so faithfuly enduring to the end. How should I bless you, if it were only for strengthening me in this blessed hope! I cling to it as a ship-wrecked ceature to the life-boat."

However, the same letter continues by teasing him for rushing off to Cheltenham to see Dr Bell on his death bed, only to be whisked off sight-seeing and to be fêted by the fashionable ladies at the spa. Dr Bell and his new system of education, in which the older children taught the younger, had deeply interested Robert and he was later to write a biography of the doctor.

He was also much occupied by his family and the precarious state of his wife's health. His daughter Edith was engaged to John Wood Warter who was training for the priesthood. Robert took her to stay with her prospective in-laws whom he greatly liked and admired - Mr Warter senior ran a school of excellent reputation, but he cannot help admitting wistfully to Caroline, "You may well suppose the visit did not exhilarate me while it lasted and I did not leave Edith there without feeling that she seemed already to belong rather to that family than to me." His wife was for the moment in better spirits, though Bertha's health worried him.

Beyond the confines of Greta Hall, great things were astir, with a tide of reform sweeping the country. The Whig government was trying to bring in a bill to reform the corrupt voting system. Over fifty boroughs returning two members each were to be disenfranchised and fifty more to lose one member out of two. It passed its second reading by a majority of one, but was later defeated and parliament dissolved. A new parliament introduced a second reform bill. When this was thrown out by the House of Lords, the whole country was in an uproar, with mobs of rioters milling about the streets - in Bristol they burned down the Mansion House and in Nottingham, the Castle.

Some months later Caroline wrote to Robert, "An officer yesterday told me he had just read the copy of a military statement by which it appears that there is good reason for supposing the Bristol affair was part of an extended plan of simultaneous rising between Birmingham, Manchester and other cities, together with the Merthyr Tydfil people; that communication had been ascertained to have been carried out by means of carrier pigeons and that the quick march of troops upon Bristol, and some towards Merthyr alone stopped the advance of an immense body of the latter."

Meanwhile the unrepresented poor were suffering outbreaks of cholera, one of them in Southampton. Seeing Robert largely through

Caroline's eyes, he does tend to take on a saintly tinge, but his comments on the outbreak show that outside his circle of friends, family and class, he was not the kindliest of men. "My brother tells me that no house could be better situated than this in case of pestilence. No doubt the pestilence will make its way over the island. We might consider ourselves here in as little danger as in any place, if it were possible to exclude vagrants from the town, the common carriers of all infectious diseases. I am one of the Board of Health, and at my suggestion all that we can do is being done to prevent these miserable pests of society from being harboured here, as they have hitherto been."

Though it is obvious from their correspondence that Caroline took a keen interest in politics, it was not until 1833 that she became really emotionally involved - then it was in the plight of children in the north. Once her feelings were roused, she turned to her only weapon, her pen, writing to Robert early in 1833, "Dear friend, will you be at the trouble of overlooking the accompanying verses? I have been reading the accounts of the factory atrocities and proofs of them taken in evidence before the House of Commons, that worked me up to a fever of indignation, which vented itself in verse. And I have a half formed plan of publishing them with some notes annexed from the minutes of evidence. But I should be glad of some encouragement from you, if you can give it me or thankful for discouragement if my attempt deserves no better. I fancy if published soon the trifle might be successful."

Caroline wanted to support Thomas Sadler who had been fighting to bring before parliament the Factories Regulation Bill, the very terms of which seem to us horrific, but they actually represented a major step forward in compassionate thinking. If the bill were passed children would work *only* ten hours a day during the week, with eight hours on Saturdays: night work was to be abolished and no child was to work under the age of nine.

Robert himself had already drawn attention to the dreadful conditions to be found in Yorkshire and Lancashire especially. "The London workhouses supplied children by wagon loads: a new sort of slave trade has been invented," he had written in an essay, also quoting a John Hunter, who swore that the conditions in the textile factories would breed new kinds of disease. Of course Robert loved and respected children, had never, with all the cares of Greta Hall, been too busy to spend time with his own, so altogether, Caroline's new project met with warm approval. He wrote back with characteristic speed and understanding, "Print your poems by all means. This is a most painful and most true one, and cannot but be felt at this time, when it is of the greatest importance that the nation should be made to feel. You have written like yourself. I could not find any words that would express higher praise."

Caroline then set to work, wrote one further poem in the form of a dramatic scene, added some quotes from Robert's essays and sent them to Blackwood together with some of the minutes of evidence which had so disturbed her in the first place. Mr Blackwood replied that he would gladly print them immediately, both in the magazine and in a small volume. Such was the enviable speed of publishing in those days that Caroline asked Mr Blackwood to correct the proofs himself, as there would not be time for them to traverse the length of England twice. Even so, she sent him a stern note on March 19th. "As it is now more than a month since I sent you *Tales of the Factories*, I think it advisable to make some enquiries." The *Tales* were published at the beginning of April.

What did Robert really think of these verses?

With kindness and tact, he says she writes like herself and of course he has great sympathy with the subject matter, but poetry they are not, a far cry from the elegant and charming pastoral verse of *The Birthday*. The *Tales* are deeply sentimental, with a piling on of agony which blunts the reader's response, not unlike the stories which were to appear later in the century about the plight of poor urban children - *Froggy's Little Brother*, or *Jessica's First Prayer.* Nevertheless they were powerful propaganda for the cause, and should be judged as such.

The Father's Tale describes the burial of a child by its remaining family - all of them deformed or deranged by working in a cotton mill.

The second, *The Grandmother's Tale* is perhaps the best of the three, at least starting on a cheerful note to add some contrast of mood. The grandmother tells how her four grandchildren were sent off by the parish to work in a mill. Two die from overwork, while a third is killed in an accident.

> By some great shaft her arm was caught -
> Only one scream she gave,
> And the wheel whirled her round and round
> They told me with a crunching sound -
> Oh to my very grave
> That sound and Jeanie's dying scream
> Will go with me...

And the fourth child is brought home to die a little more slowly.

Pestilence, the dramatic scene, takes up the idea of the mills breeding new kinds of disease, but the dead cart, houses marked with crosses and the cry 'Bring out your dead' are straight out of the Plague of London, diminishing the impact. The real dangers were harsh enough, malnutrition, exhaustion and tuberculosis. Nevertheless, the *Tales* were a brave effort to get something done by bringing dreadful conditions to light and became popular reading at that time.

Today the chief interest in *Tales of the Factories* lies in the stark, verbatim accounts of working conditions to be found at the back of the book, where Caroline is quoting the minutes of evidence taken before a committee of the House of Commons. This is part of the examination of Elizabeth Bentley.

"What time did you begin work at the factory?
When I was six years old.
What were your hours of labour in the mill?
From five in the morning till nine at night, when we were thronged. (busy)
What time was allowed for your meals?
Forty minutes at noon.
And when your work was bad you had hardly any time to eat it at all?
No, we were obliged to leave it or take it home and when we did not take it, the overseer gave it to the pigs.
Does the work keep you constantly on your feet?
Yes, there are so many frames and they run so quick.
Were you strapped if you were too much fatigued to keep up with the machinery?
Yes, the overlooker I was under was a very severe man.
Were the girls so struck as to leave black marks on their skin?
Yes, they have had black marks many times and their parents dare not come to him about it, they are afraid of losing their work. Sometimes he has got chain and chained them all down the room.
Were the children excessively fatigued at that time?
Yes, it was in the afternoon."

Another moving testimony came from a deformed girl.

"It was exceedingly dusty?
Yes, it was so dusty that the dust got up my lungs and the work was so hard. When I pulled the baskets down, I pulled my bones out of their places. It was a great basket that stood higher than this table a good deal.

How heavy was it?

I cannot say: it was a very large one that was full of weights upheaped and pulling the basket pulled my shoulder out of its place and my ribs have grown over it."

There are many more pages of this heart-rending question and answer which prompted Caroline to write her *Tales* in the first place. Many south coast readers of *Tales of the Factories* must have had only the haziest of notions beforehand as to what went on in northern textile mills, and the bare facts of the depositions, which had originally moved strong men to tears, must have reached a far wider audience as part of her book than they would ever have done as mere House of Commons evidence. So whatever it lacked in poetry, the book was a powerful call for reform.

Soon Caroline was writing to William Blackwood, thanking him for the arrival of *Tales*, and their friendly relationship was restored. He still sent her parcels of books and never failed to post a free copy of his magazine every month, which Caroline had bound up into a volume at the end of each year. The Parliamentary Reform Bill was finally passed in 1832, but it was to be a long time before child labour was brought to an end. The great textile mills of the north had done away with hand weaving and spinning on which the cottagers had depended for their livelihood: now to make ends meet they had not only to flock to the factories for work, but to send their children as well.

After the publication of *Tales of the Factories*, William Blackwood asked her for 'a cheerful title', but she replied that a long period of nursing a sick cousin at Calshot had left her quite unable to compose anything light-hearted. Yet her letters to Robert are full of delightful pictures of small domestic joys. "Spite of cats, a family of nightingales has been reared this summer, almost under my window, by the parent birds who took up their abode in the little front garden close to the house immediately upon their arrival in April. The first notice I had of my welcome guests was the song of the male as he hovered in seeming rapture over a rose bush covered with early flowers close to my window. The pair brought up four young ones, and trained them mostly, when they first left the nest, on a pink thorn under my bedroom window, where I was many a half-hour longer in dressing than usual and one morning when I came down to breakfast, one of the bold little creatures that had found its way into the house, flew over my shoulder, nothing daunted, nor farther than to his family on the thorn close by."

Robert was in need of cheer and comfort, for his wife, Edith's, decline into deep depression was a dark cloud ever more threatening. "My brother, the Doctor, thank God seems now to be recovered. His death would have brought on me a world of cares: and those from another quarter, which we now divide, would then have come upon me with a weight which it would have been impossible for me to support." Later he conjures a vision, not for the first time, of himself and Caroline together in Heaven, as near a declaration of love as circumstance would allow, a letter that any woman would treasure, yet when Edith's madness could no longer be managed at home, he is genuinely heartbroken. "Forty years has she been the life of my life and I have left her this day in a lunatic asylum."

Edith was commited to The Retreat, a hospital for the insane in York, ironically, considering Robert's opinion of William Howitt and his views, run by Quakers. As a further irony, he was deep in writing a life of William Cowper, that gentle poet whose own life had been disrupted by periods of insanity. (Caroline was later to be described as 'the Cowper of our modern poetesses', by the *Quarterly Review*)

In the same year, William Blackwood died and Caroline lost a real friend. Though his son Alexander wrote with assurances that her work would still be welcome, relations were never the same. When Alexander followed his brothers to India - and Caroline had written asking Captain

Bruce to befriend yet another Blackwood - the magazine stopped coming. The correspondence became merely a business one, though it was not even business-like, for at one time a letter of hers was not answered for a year! Once this would have seemed like the end of the world, but Robert's warm encouragement over the years had bred a certain confidence in herself. She was hard at work on the final part of *The Birthday.*

She continued to draw, also. Robert had asked for a portrait and she had sent him one with the huge dog Mufti languishing against her knees, staring soulfully up into her face. At forty seven, Caroline is bird-like, small boned with pointed features, dark eyes, her hair drawn up in an elegant knot, her slender person dressed in a flowing, gauzy gown nipped in to a small waist, with a shawl collar and leg o'mutton sleeves. Robert was delighted with it, proclaiming it a very good likeness. (see illustration)

With all the cares of Edith's illness he had not been able to go off on his usual round of visits, so had not seen the real Caroline for three years. Edith improved sufficiently to be brought home to Greta Hall in 1835. Henry paid them a visit and wrote afterwards, "Robert appears to bear his calamity better than I could have imagined. His daughter Kate is of course depressed and nervous, but not more so than is quite natural under the circumstances. As for Edith herself, she is in a state approaching fatuity from which there is no chance of her ever recovering."

Robert's friend Wordsworth was also giving cause for alarm. Caroline wrote anxiously inquiring if the newspaper report were true that he was in danger of losing his sight. Robert replied, "The account of Wordsworth's eyes was true; they have been saved for the present. But for many years he has been subject to inflammation of the lids, and when this extends to the eye, the sight is seriously endangered and there is always danger of new attacks, where an inflammatory habit has once been formed. Any emotion immediately affects the diseased part; the excitement of conversation is sufficient for the evil; and by composing two sonnets during the last attack he had nealy brought on a relapse." Though it was many years now since Caroline had met the Wordsworths, Dora still kept in touch with her, shared news of the infamous William Howitt, and sent her books.

At the beginning of 1836, Robert wrote, "When I may be able to leave home again, God only knows. My presence is necessary here and there is no likelihood of any improvement that might render it prudent for me to be absent. We are thankful when the days pass quietly." That was a terrible sentence; Caroline was to recall it all too painfully in later years.

At present, it was a difficult period for her to bear. She could only go on writing and waiting for Robert's letters. So they continued with the usual tender inquiries after each other's health and work, literary gossip, opinions on books and politics. Caroline had a new little spaniel, Dashie, ready to defend her to the death. Robert was finishing the third volume of his life of William Cowper, though with all his cares, never too busy to write to her.

By the autumn there was better news; with Kate and her sister Bertha now able to manage looking after their mother, Robert planned a long journey round England, taking Cuthbert with him and would visit Caroline. The spring returned to her step. In September he wrote, "I think of cutting out some work, or rather of setting some aside to be done at Buckland as in 1831, so I shall just show Cuthbert to you, send him on to Tarring, and follow after him in a few days." This was still four months ahead, but it gave Caroline immense pleasure to look forward - she had not seen Robert for nearly five years.

He and Cuthbert set out at the beginning of November, staying with his old friend and publisher, Joseph Cottle in Bristol, meeting fellow poet Walter Savage Landor, then visiting William Lisle Bowles, after which they travelled almost to Land's End to see Derwent Coleridge, now a curate at Helston. "Christmas I expect to pass with my dear old friend Lightfoot, near Crediton, and New Year's Day most probably with you," he wrote to Caroline from Bedminster. "My accounts from home could not be more favourable. My first letter produced an expression of some interest in its contents; my absence occasions no uneasiness, and my return will, I dare say, be looked for with as much pleasure as my poor Edith is now capable of finding in anything."

So Robert came to Buckland once more, meeting Caroline after long absence with the ease of an old friend, sitting by the fire in the small, panelled living room, exchanging news, both deeply happy in each other's company. Behind the tall, leafless elms, in this peaceful cottage, Robert was able to catch up on some writing, editing William Cowper's collected poems, reviewing for the *Quarterly Review*, always an important part of his workload, and preparing his own poems for a new, large edition which his publishers had decided to bring out. Their old scheme of writing *Robin Hood* together was resurrected and discussed again, though it made slow progress. After the strain of living with Edith's insanity, Caroline's understanding and loving care for his work touched him deeply - part of him wanted to stay on at Buckland.

Robert's daughter Edith-May had married John Wood Warter, now appointed curate at Tarring in West Sussex. When Cuthbert had gone on ahead to stay with his sister, Robert and Caroline were alone. All his life, Robert had carried on a wide and voluminous correspondence, at once a pleasure and a burden. A bundle of letters had been sent on from Greta Hall to await him at Buckland, one of them echoing Caroline's own first pages nearly twenty years ago, from a young woman asking advice about a writing career.

Robert replied, "Do not suppose I disparage the gift which you possess; nor that I would discourage you from exercising it. I only exhort you so to think of it, and so to use it, as to render it conducive to your own permanent good. Write poetry for its own sake not in the spirit of emulation and with a view to celebrity; the less you aim at that, the more likely you will be to deserve and finally to obtain it." He went on to remind her that a woman's place is primarily in the home. Her name was Charlotte Brontë...

In between working sessions, Robert and Caroline went for wintry walks with Dash, the dog, round the quiet lanes, Caroline on her small pony Oberon, to come home and sit by the logwood fire while Robert described all his recent travels and Caroline showed him her latest poems. Her devotion to Robert had not been in question for many years now, but for the first time it is plain that Robert loves Caroline deeply, for when it comes to parting, he cannot endure it, is even driven to say perhaps they should not plan to meet again because the pain of parting was unbearable.

Fortunately for her own state of mind, Caroline did not take this too seriously, though she hated the first empty days after Robert had gone. At least she could write and look forward to his letters. Soon after he left, she wrote, "Sorely and sadly I have missed you, and shall miss you, till that feeling of deprivation softens into one of grateful and pleasant introspection, such as I have learnt to live upon and be thankful. I will not agree with you that it may be better never to meet then only to part. The next pleasure I shall have will be to hear you are in your haven again and that your return home and the welcome of your dear daughters has been as little saddened as possible under the cloud with which it pleases God still to overshadow you. I must tell you that Dashie has felt your departure very sensibly; I found him the next day scratching at your bedroom door; and when my solitary dinner was brought up to me on a tray, he rushed down again and bounced open the bedroom door, barking with all his might to call you to partake."

At Easter Robert wrote of Charlotte Brontë, "I sent a dose of cooling admonition to the poor girl whose flighty letter reached me at Buckland. It was well taken and she thanked me for it. It seems she is the eldest daughter of a clergyman, has been expensively educated and is laudably employed as a governess in some private family. About the same time that she wrote to me, her brother wrote to Wordsworth, who was disgusted with the letter, for it contained gross flattery to him, and plenty of abuse of other poets, including me. I think well of the sister from her second letter and probably she will think kindly of me so long as she lives."

Perhaps the office of Poet Laureate allows one to be so smug! Caroline's own longest work, *The Birthday* had recently been published, receiving mixed reviews, one magazine describing it as doggerel verse. But Henry Nelson Coleridge, somewhat later, was to write in the *Quarterly Review*, "She has much of that great writer, Cowper's, humour, fondness for rural life, melancholy pathos and moral satire. She has also Cowper's pre-eminently English manner in diction and thought. We do not remember any recent author whose poetry is so unmixed native; and this English complexion constitutes one of its characteristic charms."

The Birthday is Caroline's lasting achievement, ninety pages of blank verse handled with great technical skill so that it never grows monotonous, but flows on, long lines and short, dialogue and narrative, taking the reader with it. Though she is looking back upon a much loved time, she can do so now with deep pleasure rather than grief, often laughing gently at her own young self. There are delightful and detailed character sketches of the gardener and his wife, glimpses of her family, long descriptions of all her pets and their antics, set within her beloved garden or the green countryside of Buckland.

Only occasionally is it marred, at least to twentieth century ears, by lines of moralising, say on field sports, or poverty. There is one curious passage quite outside the Buckland scene, in which she recalls visiting a London prison and talking to a prisoner making jewellery who has brought in an orchid in a pot, to have one wild green reminder of the country. This seems totally outside the probable experience of fourteen year old Caroline. Was it yet one more of her grandmother's tales, which moved her imagination? The long poem ends with a description of a visit to the Rev. Gilpin - *The Birthday* is a distillation of childhood equalled only by Wordsworth's *Prelude*: no other poem in the language details so elegantly and humourously the trials and pleasures of a child growing up. One is bound to wish that it continued, unravelling the mysteries of her teens, but as it is, ending before the death of her father, it achieves an artistic unity which might otherwise have been spoiled.

Edward Dowden gives some extracts from *The Birthday*, and praises four of her tragic narrative poems, *The Young Grey Head, The Murder Glen, Walter and William,* and *The Evening Walk*, likening them to the best of Crabbe - "a Crabbe in whom womanly tenderness replaces the hard veracity characteristic of that eminent poet." Unfortunately for Caroline's reputation, these doom laden chronicles, though technically brilliant in their use of the rhyming couplet and often deeply moving, are not to present day taste. *The Birthday* though has a timeless quality. Short quotations hardly reveal this. Here is the beginning of the fishing expedition described in Chapter One.

> That was a lovely brook, by whose green marge
> We two, the patient angler and his child,
> Loitered away so many summer days!
> A shallow sparkling stream, it hurried, now
> Leaping and glancing among large round stones,
> With everlasting friction chafing still
> Their polished smoothness, on a gravelly bed
> Then softly slipped away with rippling sound,
> Or all inaudible where the green moss

Sloped down to meet the clear reflected wave
That lipped its emerald bank with seeming show
Of gentle dalliance; in a dark, deep pool
Collected now, the peaceful waters slept,
Embayed by rugged headlands, hollow roots
Of huge old pollard willows. Anchored there,
Rode safe from every gale a sylvan fleet
Of milk-white water lilies, every bark
Worthy as those on his own sacred flood
To waft the Indian Cupid. Then the stream
Brawling again o'er pebbly shallows ran
On, to where a rustic, rough-hewn bridge
All bright with mosses and green ivy wreaths
Spanned the small channel with its single arch;
And underneath the bank on either side
Shelved down into the water, darkly green
With unsunned verdure, or whereon the sun
Looked only when his rays at eventide
Obliquely glanced between the blackened piers
With arrowy beams of emerald light
Touching the river and its velvet marge.
Twas there, beneath the archway, just within
Its rough, misshapen piles, I found a cave.
A little secret cell - one large flat stone
Its ample floor, imbedded deep in moss,
And a rich tuft of dark blue violet
And fretted o'er with curious groining dark,
Like vault of Gothic chapel, was the roof
Of that small cunning cave - "The Naiad's Grot"
   ... So methought

> The little Naiad of our brook might haunt
> That cool retreat, and to her guardian care
> My wont was ever, at the bridge arrived
> To trust our basket, with its simple store
> Of home-made, wholesome cakes, by one at home
> Provided for our banquet hour at noon.
>
> A joyful hour! anticipated keen ...
> The busy, bustling joy, with housewife airs
> Directress, handmaid, lady of the feast -
> To spread that 'table in the wilderness'!
> The spot selected with deliberate care,
> Where all was beautiful; some pleasant nook
> Among the fringeing alders, or beneath
> A single spreading oak, or higher up
> Within the thicket, a more secret bower
> A little clearing, carpeted all o'er
> With creeping strawberry, and greenest moss,
> Thick veined with ivy.

Perhaps the publication of this major work made Caroline feel more generous, for she had a change of heart over the servant girl poet, Mary Colling, wrote to her mistress, Mrs Bray, and actually sent a book for Mary, rejoicing in their common love of flowers. Anna Bray wrote cordially in return inviting her to come and stay at Tavistock, if she were ever in Devon

In the November of that year, Robert's wife died; in this case the cliché, 'a happy release' was fully justified, since poor Edith had known only grief and depression since the death of Belle. Even so, Robert mourned her deeply. Caroline must have wondered what difference this would make to her relationship with Robert, but his letter to her a fortnight after Edith's death must have quelled any hope of an early visit.

"Winter has begun with us unusually early, and it is as cold now as in the ordinary course of seasons it is at Christmas. This, however, is better than the heavy storms of wind and rain which preceded this frost and rendered it impossible for Bertha and Kate to get out of doors. Yesterday was the first day they could walk out. Their health, thank God, has not suffered and at their time of life their spirits, in the wise order of nature, have a tendency to recover their healthy tone. For myself, truly and deeply thankful as I ought to be and am, for a deliverance which has long been desired, I continually feel the separation. I never felt wholly like myself anywhere but at home, and the change is so great that I no longer feel like myself there. This, however, will be the best place for me for some time to come, so that if it were convenient for me in other respects to move, I should deem it advisable to let some months elapse before I commenced a journey."

This sounds harsh, after his tender parting with Caroline in January; obviously he was still shocked with grief, which she would have been the first to understand. His reading of his daughters' health, on the other hand, was to prove highly over-optimistic.

A further letter early in the new year is also totally impersonal as far as Caroline is concerned. It discusses Warner's *Recollections*, a book which she had lent him, and the state of the railways.

But when the shock of Edith's death had worn off a little, Robert began to realise how lonely he was. His daughter Bertha had recently married her cousin, Herbert Hill; Edith-May, his eldest, lived far away in Sussex; Cuthbert was mostly away now, studying, so only Kate was at home. The large rooms of Greta Hall which had seethed with the activity of so many young Coleridges and Southeys now echoed with emptiness. (The Coleridges were long gone, Sara to marry her cousin Henry, Mrs Coleridge to live with Derwent in Cornwall: Hartley had become a wanderer and Samuel Coleridge had died in 1834) Also he was becoming noticeably absent-minded. He tried to carry on writing, always his solace, planning a three volume life of Dr Andrew Bell, the educational reformer whom he admired so much, but work was not enough. His thoughts returned to Caroline. Robert was sixty four, Caroline fifty two.

Edward Dowden wrote, "When after change and grievous loss at home, when he dared to look forward to a quiet eventide of toil, he found that his friend of twenty years, whose age approached his own, and whose sympathy with his thoughts and strivings was constantly and instinctively right, would be the truest and most helpful companion for the close of his life. Making no break with the past, he might draw the bonds of friendship tighter - he might perfect the friendship in the dearest way of all."

So at last he came to Buckland and asked Caroline to marry him. Surprisingly, she at first refused, maintaining that she could not burden him with another invalid wife, but Robert continued to plead, and in the end she agreed. Twenty one years after writing that first shy letter to the Poet Laureate, she was to become Mrs Robert Southey, her feelings a welter of love and joy, worry and apprehension - her health, leaving beloved Buckland after fifty years, a family of step-children, but her chief concern was to make Robert happy once more.

She had plenty of leisure to consider the future, for Robert spent the summer travelling in Europe with Cuthbert, his friend Henry Crabb Robinson and several others.

On his return Robert and Caroline were married at Boldre, in June 1839, in the little stone church on its wooded knoll above Lymington River, which she had described so well in *Chapter on Churchyards*.

Robert wrote to Walter Savage Landor, "Reduced in number as my famiy has been these last few years, my spirits would hardly recover their habitual and healthy cheerfulness, if I had not prevailed upon Miss Bowles to share my lot for the remainder of our lives. There is just such a disparity of age as is fitting. We have been well acquainted with each other more than twenty years and a more perfect conformity of disposition could not exist, so that in resolving upon what must be either the weakest or the wisest act of a sexegenarian's life, I am well assured, according to human foresight I have judged well and acted wisely, both for myself and for my remaining daughter."

The rest of the summer was spent at Buckland, perhaps the happiest time of Caroline's whole life - certainly her health greatly improved. Much of the time was spent in visiting her relations, at Calshot Castle, the Burrards at Walhampton, at all of which Robert was most warmly received and welcomed. He took a great interest in this new family circle, inviting the Burrard girls to come and stay in Keswick, while Caroline immensely enjoyed showing him off. And why not? Robert had kept his slim figure and though his hair was white, he was still a handsome man, moreover he was one of the most famous writers in England, and the Poet Laureate.

Her relatives did notice that he was growing rather forgetful, but this was charitably described as mere absence of mind, such as you might expect from a distinguished poet.

chapter eight

We came together at life's eventide

So, seventeen years after her one visit there, Caroline came back to Greta Hall, this time as its mistress. No house could be a greater contrast with Buckland Cottage, which was let, than this tall building with its curved, tower-like wings, lofty rooms and high windows overlooking the roofs of Keswick, with great mountains looming over it - at least they must have seemed great after the flat, tamed countryside bordering the New Forest, mountains "as fantastic as if Nature had laughed herself into the convulsion in which they were made," Coleridge had written of his view.

They arrived on August 31st, as Caroline reported to Blackwood's, though her writing desk, books and personal goods and chattels had been sent on by sea and had still not appeared by September 19th.

Caroline had fallen in love with the landscape on her previous visit, so she was prepared for its strangeness. She was used to Robert's constant company now and delighted in it. What she was not in the least prepared for was the attitude of the household at Greta Hall, which comprised Robert's sister-in-law, Mary Lovell, Cuthbert, now twenty one and at Oxford, and Kate, who was thirty.

Mary Lovell, with whom Caroline had fancied there was a bond in their common love of flowers and gardening, kept to herself. Cuthbert was very different from the boy to whom she had sent countless jokey messages about cats, though fortunately not a great deal at home. Kate, quite simply, hated her step-mother.

Reading between the lines of Robert's description of that long ago picnic sketch, it is possible to hear the young Southey girls giggling together over Caroline; obviously the younger ones had never taken to her, since all the subsequent messages to and fro had been from Cuthbert. To be fair to Kate, she'd had a most difficult life, losing her beloved sister, Belle, only two years her junior, when she was fifteen, then watching her mother slowly descending into madness, being confined to an asylum, returning home to become totally insane and reliant upon her family. Then Kate and Cuthbert had largely been looked after by the eldest sister, Edith-May. Now Edith and Bertha were married, so Kate had been left alone to run the house for her father whom she adored, and naturally had become his close companion after her mother's death. Then he had absented himself, leaving her alone, for some months while he stayed at Buckland and now into her life comes Caroline, in place of her dear mother.

Wordsworth described how Robert had written to Edith and Bertha in October the previous year, telling them of his engagement to Caroline. "This intelligence was a shock to them - how could it be otherwise. They were wearing deep mourning for their mother who had not been buried twelve months, and whom they had watched day and night during the long melancholy disease which preceded her dissolution. In addition to this, I observed that those considerations and feelings which naturally indispose grown up daughters to look favourably upon their father's second marriage, affected them more than was to be wished; and thinking their notions upon second marriages were not sufficiently enlarged, I took much pains to set them right upon the subject, and I can safely say, not without success.

In justice to Kate, I must here add she frequently said, that if her father were to marry again, Miss Bowles was of all persons from what she had heard and seen of her in her writings, the one whom she would prefer."

Surely Robert's mental powers must already have been impaired, or he would have treated his own children with far more sensitivity. As it was, he had written ingenuously to Caroline, "Cuthbert you know loves you already, and it would be the delight of Kate, once she has recovered from the first natural feeling, to receive you as friend and companion." Kate had indeed written to Caroline, addressing her astonishingly, as Dear Mother. But a few days after her actual arrival at Greta Hall, Kate was demanding, "How could you believe that any grown up children could approve of their father's taking a second wife?" She also wrote to her sisters describing Caroline in the most hostile terms, noting, "the disagreeable impression caused by her unprepossessing appearance and the rough manner of the intruder."

Whether Caroline realised it or not, Robert's health had begun to deteriorate during his long stay at Buckland. It was natural that Kate and Cuthbert should blame her not only for this, but for keeping him away from home so long and for leaving them in the dark about his state of mind.

Caroline had arrived prepared to love her step-children, and sensibly decided to leave the household management in Kate's hands, devoting herself to Robert, who was becoming more and more forgetful. When he was not working on his life of Dr Bell, he and Caroline planned a series of sonnets on the seasons written jointly, and to resurrect their old plan of writing *Robin Hood* together.

Much later, writing a preface, Caroline looked back to this time. "The dark hour had passed away. [Edith's death] At eventide, there was light and with returning cheerfulness and reviving hope, old pleasurable projects were remembered and resumed with a more confident expectation on both sides. *Robin Hood* was shortly to be taken in hand in good earnest and in the meantime it was our design to publish, in one volume my still uncollected poems with some of my beloved husband's. *March* was to have formed one of a series entitled *The Calendar*, of which we were to have written the months alternately. It was a pleasant dream..."

In spite of her delicate health, Caroline could walk four or five miles, so they would go for expeditions over Catbells, up Skiddaw, to Watendlath, or shorter ones to the lakeside and Friar's Crag. Her life was now totally bound up with Robert's. She wrote little of her own and made no friends outside Greta Hall. Robert seemed not to notice Kate's hostility and Caroline tried to shrug it off, enjoying the times when Kate was away, staying with one of her married sisters, happy in the knowledge that Robert himself was happy once more, busy writing, walking and talking over with her all their old plans. For a few months her married life was content enough for her own health to improve.

But Robert's deteriorated.

He was becoming more and more absent-minded, spent long periods staring into space when he should have been writing, though physically still strong enough. At first Caroline tried to keep this state secret from his friends, but by the beginning of 1840, it was plain that his mind was in some way affected: Robert, who had written millions of words during his lifetime, could no longer write.

Faced with a hostile household where the only friendly face was her maid, Honor, whom she had brought from Buckland, Caroline turned to Anna Bray in far away Tavistock as one of her chief confidantes; it was a measure of her loneliness that she should be driven to this, for the two women had never met. From the tone of her letters, the reader would guess that Caroline was writing to a mother-figure, but Anna was in fact four years her junior. She had certainly known her own share of sorrow and always wrote back with much warmth and sympathy.

Anna had married Charles Stothard, an artist working on a nation wide illustrated catalogue of sculptured monuments, and travelled with him, till he was killed by falling off a ladder whilst drawing in Beer Ferrars church in 1821. Anna's child, born soon after, lived only seven months. Later she married Edward Bray, the vicar of Tavistock, and settled down to writing novels; one of these, *The Moor of Portugal*, had brought her in touch with Robert, an authority on that country and thence to Caroline. Robert had encouraged her to seek out Devon folklore which she often used in her books; later she wrote a whole series of novels based on the history of West Country families, which were highly popular, though being a prolific novelist never prevented her sending punctual and concerned replies to Caroline's letters.

Perhaps it was *because* they had never met that Caroline felt able to pour out her heart on Robert's illness and the whole troubled state of things at Greta Hall. Since she insisted on looking after Robert all the time, his illness which might have brought her and Kate closer together, only drove them further apart, whilst Cuthbert grew ever more resentful of the way the family was being excluded.

On New Year's Day Caroline wrote to Anna, "Would to find I could give such accounts of my beloved husband as I know you are sincerely desirous to receive. But the best I can say of him is this, that I do not think any material change in his state has taken place for the last four months - which little there is, is not alas! for the better. When I compare him with what he was at the time of our marriage in June last, my heart sickens at the alteration. No serious apprehensions came upon me until some time after our marriage and then I hoped and believed, in common with his brother, Dr Southey, that our journey hitherward and the reviving influence of his own mountain air would affect his complete restoration. But the enfeebled body 'presseth down' the once healthful mind, though without affecting its rationality in the slightest manner. The latent power is perfect, but that of bringing it into action seems for the present withdrawn - and I believe it to proceed from a consciousness of this actual inability that Mr S voluntarily refrains from all attempts at composition - even from letter writing. He talks as cheerfully and with as much confidence as ever of resuming his literary labours . . . My dear husband's pleasure in his books is unabated and he reads to me - and with me - a great part of every day - when the weather is favourable he takes walking exercise with me to the extent of four or five miles... There is good hope (his brother thinks) that all will be right again.

It has been a matter of regret to me that many of his correspondents - under the erroneous idea of his state probably - have altogether ceased writing to him."

In a postscript she reveals her total devotion to Robert - and what must to Kate have seemed possessiveness. "You will excuse a hastily written letter, written as regards contents under some restraint in the presence of Mr S, from whom I am never absent a quarter of an hour at a time out of the twenty four." One can only feel compassion for Kate, brought up in a large, loving family, never strong in health herself, having lost the company of her mother, sisters and even Cuthbert for most of the time. Now in effect she loses her father to this intruding stranger. Deep bitterness spread through the household, affecting even the servants.

Caroline had at least remained on good terms with the eldest daughter, Edith-May, now living in West Sussex with her husband, John Warter. ("She is her Father's own child in all respects") Caroline hoped they would come to stay in the summer, both to relieve the tension and to rouse Robert.

At the end of February, Caroline wrote to Anna Bray thanking her for her warmth and concern. "You would see Mr S sadly changed in person, though he was not looking well when you saw him - but last year he had so wonderfully recovered his good looks... that this latter falling away is the more perceptible and painful to me. His appetite is however tolerable and he has no bodily suffering nor specific disease. I long for summer with the fearful longing of a last hope and I have felt myself so failing lately that sometimes the dread comes upon me that I may not last out while he wants me."

After this cry from the heart there is some good family news. Bertha, now Mrs Herbert Hill, has a fine baby daughter and her husband has just been inducted to the curacy of Rydal, close to his home.

When Robert had returned from his West Country travels in 1838, Cuthbert had stayed at Buckland Cottage for a week, before going on to Edith-May, so that Caroline had enjoyed getting to know, and indeed, to like him as a young man, not having seen him since he was in frocks. He had made an easy guest, laughing and joking with her maid, Honor, and generally impressing her as the true son of his father.

But Cuthbert as step-son was very different, in league with Kate against her. "It would have given Robert quiet pleasure if Cuthbert would sometimes have spent an hour with him in reading some foreign language, but the young man so greatly differs from his father in his distaste to study and strong addiction to all field sports, that when he is at home he cannot find time for bookish occupation. I hope he may be more diligent at Oxford - but he has been too much his own master from a boy . . . He has excellent abilities and I hope and believe good principles. His sister idolises him and can see no fault in him - having in fact trained him up herself on more levelling and democratic principles than quite beseems Mr Southey's children. These young people have grown up under grave disadvantages since the removal of their eldest sister - the prop and mainstay of the house."

One might have expected Caroline to make a friend of Mary Lovell, who was outside the main feud, as it were, near her own age and according to her contemporaries, a woman of wit and culture. Edward Quillinan, Dora Wordsworth's husband, wrote, "Mrs Lovell dined with Miss Fenwick and was really lively and entertaining. She had read all the odd books in Southey's library and has an excellent memory so that she can apply many queer and pleasant illustrations to the chance topics of social talk "

But in the same letter to Anna, Caroline wrote, "I see little of Kate or Cuthbert or Mrs Lovell their aunt, except at dinner and supper, as it has never been Mr Southey's custom to sit with his family except at meals and now he is never quite comfortable except when alone with me in his study." So it was little wonder that Cuthbert no longer felt welcomed by his own father if this was the state of affairs - at least in Caroline's eyes. She even complained that, egged on by his sister, Cuthbert had threatened to strike her.

It was the affair of Honor's leg which brought about the longest outpouring to Anna Bray. Almost as soon as they arrived, Honor had been forced to take to her bed with an inflamed leg. "For months I have been her sick nurse, dressing her leg twice daily, helping her to dress and undress, make her bed - even her fire, till I insisted on having a person as Nurse who gave directions they dare not disobey - I know no one out of this house - completely in their toils ... Now I hope the poor creature is slowly recovering. I shall at least soon have the comfort of her services and of meeting her as I move about the house - one face at least that I can lift my eyes to without a sinking heart."

One can not but feel sympathy for the whole household, rent with such bitterness, and especially for Kate who had been close to her father for thirty years, whereas Caroline was a mere newcomer. She feels Kate's hatred as the black core of the house and it is obvious that her pride is deeply hurt. Kate and Cuthbert have not treated her with respect - she even calls Kate undisciplined as if forgetting she is a grown woman. Even her sensible plan for leaving the housekeeping in Kate's hands, did not work in practice.

"No doubt had the poor father been himself, a very different line of conduct would have been pursued, though I do not think the deep hatred conceived for his second wife could have been conceded. But at least I should have had a protector. My desire was to leave the household management as I found it, in the hands of Miss Southey and her upper servant - and I did so - without a single act of interference - though from the first I was treated with indignity, till I was compelled by necessity and duty to my husband to assume the management of his affairs. I have struggled on as I could, securing to him at least, comforts he would otherwise be wholly deprived of, this at a cost to myself which would, before this have been that of life, I think."

This was again written to Anna Bray, but she wrote similar letters to her friend Mrs Hughes, who was known to Henry Crabb Robinson, one of Wordsworth's closest correspondents, so her complaints filtered back to the family and Wordsworth himself was drawn into the feud as chief mediator. Though he would naturally incline to Kate, having known her all her life and seen a great deal of her as his daughter Dora's friend, he turned first to her, to persuade her to take a more charitable view of her step-mother, urging patience and resignation.

Mary Wordsworth, who was equally fond of Kate, then called on Caroline, who at once brought up the subject of the family discord and speaking in great distress of mind, begged Mary and the Wordsworth family to judge her with kindness. William at once felt that he must pay a visit and found Caroline extremely agitated. William did his utmost to appear fair minded, pointing out where he thought Kate had been mistaken and over emotional. "Mrs Southey took in good part every question I thought it expedient to put to her, and more than this - she entreated me to cross-question her, that was her very expression. In several points with which I had been dissatisfied and especially in her not having communicated to Mr Southey's daughters the state of body and mind in which their Father had been during his residence in Miss Bowles' house before his marriage - and their protracted sojourn there after that event, she gave explanations to me that were most acceptable, as removing much of the blame I had previously attached to her conduct (before her marriage) as evincing an error of judgement, if not want of feeling. But upon the whole the interview was sadly unpromising. The views she had taken of Kate's behaviour, the interpretations she had put upon her words and actions and the notions, so different from my own which she obviously entertained of her general character, extinguished, when I bore in mind Kate's sentiments whether right or wrong, towards Mrs S, the faint hope I had carried with me of being serviceable - I left the house however with a strong sympathy to Mrs S's sufferings and with an unqualified pity for her, as being exposed to trials which her constitution of body and mind, conjoined with her previous position as a single lady and sole mistress of her house had made her unequal to."

All kinds of chores devolved on Caroline now, from paying bills to keeping slates on the roof. She wrote to their landlord, William Finlay Watson, an Edinburgh bookseller, apologising for being late with the rent, thirty seven pounds, ten shillings for the half year for Greta Hall and the adjacent field, which was a great trouble to her. "I am sorry to say that the Keswick people seem determined to make their way, in spite of all remonstrance, by the backway through the field at the entrance of which you erected a wall with a locked door to prevent this great nuisance. Upon my having the lock changed, they made a way through Mr Sealby's fence at the side ... a public way very detrimental to your property as well as to our great annoyance. I have also employed the police here to be on the look out - but all in vain - there now appears to be a determined effort to force a passage."

Obviously she had no time or inclination for her own writing, though she had to deal with a certain amount of literay correspondence. Ironically, her own work was growing in popularity, *Gems* from her poems having been published in America several years before. Blackwood's still asked her for short pieces and were planning to reprint *Chapters on Churchyards*, also to be published in New York in 1842. She still wrote to Blackwood's though only infrequent notes. "I would have sent a contribution for Maga, but the most afflictive causes prevented me." There were often requests to set her poems to music.

In addition there was Robert's once voluminous correspondence. To begin with, she had refused to answer personal letters to him, hoping that in the end his conscience would spur him on to the effort of writing, but soon it was evident that he would not write again. His publisher at the *Quarterly Review*, William Murray, wrote her a most kindly letter which must have comforted her sore heart. "Dear Madam. For such is to me, I can assure you, one so completely connected with the happiness of that invaluable man and I am proud to add, my old friend, Mr Southey." He went on to report sales of the latest edition of the *Book of the Church* as very satisfactory and asks if she can ascertain whether there are any suggestions for improvements to a new edition which he hoped to bring out soon. "Tell Mr S that I cherish with much gratefulness a letter which he wrote me during the fluster of Catholic Emacipation, to remain firmly to our principles at the *Quarterly Review*. Offer my kindest regards to Mr S and tell him that I still fervently hope that one who remembered his creator in the days of his youth will not be forgotten by Him in his old age."

While letters were time consuming it must have been a relief to communicate with the outside world and keep up at least a modicum of literary correspondence, considering the bleak atmosphere inside the walls of Greta Hall.

Robert's mental health continued to decline. Wordsworth came to see him one afternoon and found this man who owned twelve thousand books, sitting, smiling apparently contentedly into space and occasionally patting a book which lay on his lap, as if it were one of the household cats. Robert's brother, Henry, paid visits when he could and reported to John May, with clearer eyes than Caroline's, "Robert's bodily health - the mind is quite gone, there remains mere animal life and that may exist for a long period. He does not suffer, thank God, but his best friends must now rejoice to hear that he is released from those trammels of the flesh by which his immortal mind is now bound down."

Henry was indeed a great comfort to Caroline, someone to whom she could turn with complete confidence, not only for medical advice. Her split with Kate, Cuthbert and what she harshly refers to as the Coleridge-Clique, was now complete. Henry was on her side, together with Edith-May, her husband and the local vicar. In her letters to Anna Bray Caroline frequently prayed for strength to go on living and nursing Robert, but her deeply held religious feelings certainly failed to bring any light and love to the general situation.

Her faith in the next world, so often discussed in letters to Robert certainly bore her up at this difficult time, but it was an inward looking faith; perhaps only a saint could have reconciled the household. She had obviously gone to Keswick expecting to be treated with respect, whereas Kate, a woman of thirty, used to running the house and nursing her own mother, expected to be treated as an equal - if anyone desperately needed a loving Christian friend at this time, it was Kate.

But the feud only deepened, for Caroline found it necessary to dismiss the Southey's old family servant Betty who had been in their service for many years and had helped nurse Edith. Cuthbert was so incensed at this that he moved out of Greta Hall into lodgings in Keswick and came racing to the Wordsworths at Rydal Mount to tell them, and Kate who had taken refuge with her friends. At a family conference between Kate, Cuthbert, Bertha and her husband, they resolved to demand that Kate must be allowed to live at Greta Hall in rooms apart from Caroline's and to see her father once a day alone, which seems reasonable enough - at that time she was seeing him only once a week!

Wordworth suggested to Kate that she should write an account of what had passed between herself and Mrs Southey, largely for the benefit of her sister Edith Warter, who had sided with Caroline. The Warters paid a visit to Greta Hall at this time, which was a great pleasure for Caroline, but only deepened the divide between the sisters. Caroline had found a friend in Mr Myers, the local vicar, and on hearing of Kate's written account, or 'Recollections', she sent for him to give her own description of the situation between her and Kate. Mr Myers then went over to Rydal Mount to ask Wordsworth if he would mediate again between the two women, but he declined to be involved any further, judging the affair hopeless when such bitterness reigned on both sides. He continued to find it all a great worry, particularly with regard to Kate's welfare.

He wrote to Henry Crabb Robinson, "I was especially moved by the very delicate state of health into which Kate had been thrown by the anxiety and fatigue she underwent during her dutiful attendance on her Mother for the last three or four years of her life while she was labouring under a most affecting malady - by a severe and dangerous sickness she was herself seized with - and subsequently the ignorance she was kept in as to the condition of her Father from the twelfth of March when he left Keswick for Buckland, till the last day of August when he returned home with Mrs Southey."

In Kate's 'Recollections', Caroline felt herself to be accused of some mysterious crime presumably to do with Robert's finances. She wrote to Anna Bray, "The gentleman from hence who made so veracious a report of the conduct of my Husband's children toward me, must have been Mr Spedding - a man of law and a most respectable one - the same who (I told you) had been pitched upon as an assessor to Mr Myers, in investigating the charges against me, as personified in Miss S's 'Recollections'. Finding themselves condemned by Mr Spedding on their own representation, they then sent it up to London - with notes and annotations - and a request to their friend - formally their father's - Mr Taylor that he would send down a professional man to do . . . I never quite understood what - but I suppose to put me on trial. Mr Taylor was too much in their interest to do their bidding." [presumably she means he could see any such trial would fail]

Robert had once claimed Henry Taylor as his best friend among the younger generation. Author of several verse tragedies, he had eventually entered the Colonial Office, but kept up his literary interests by writing reviews for the *Quarterly*. He had visited Holland with Robert in 1826. Robert's will appointed him literary executor and he set up a board of trustees to look after the interests of the Southey children.

There were lighter moments when Caroline describes the beauty of the lake below, the encircling mountains and the balmy air, though she cannot walk far and leave Robert. What did cheer her immensely was the prospect of her two Burrard cousins coming to stay, women she had looked upon almost as sisters all her life. In the winter there was a visit from Edith-May of whom she was growing increasingly fond.

It was seldom that she had time, inclination or mental energy to write. Even if the impulse came, she would not usually indulge it, for writing poetry had always been a welling up of emotion and this she felt unable to afford, until Robert's birthday in 1841, when she wrote a sonnet.

> Sixty and seven hast thou fulfilled this day
> My husband, of the appointed years of men;
> Now resting from thy labours a brief span
> Before the final close. I dare not pray
> That the mysterious veil be drawn away
> Which parts thee from this world and all its woes.

Another sonnet survives from this time, addressed to the face in an old family portrait -

> ... thy sweet patience teach
> To thy sad daughter, in her strange estate
> So tired - so mated, yet so desolate

Blackwood's suggested, as her writing was now so popular that, lacking any new work, they should reprint her very first long poem, *Ellen Fitzarthur*; she wrote back firmly suggesting they reprint *The Widow's Tale* as well, in a separate volume. Her letters to Blackwood always show a most business-like attitude. They agreed to publish *The Widow's Tale* and she replied tartly, "As you consider it advisable to put my two little volumes into one, I can only acquiesce - though I cannot like the clumsy thickness of the form."

By 1842, Robert's invalid state had become an accepted part of life and was no longer news. The household likewise had calmed down since Caroline was obviously there to stay. Cuthbert was busy preparing to take Holy Orders and his thoughts were elsewhere - he had become engaged. Kate, who had returned from taking refuge with the Wordsworths, was often away staying with friends or her sisters. Caroline's letters, although Robert was always lovingly mentioned, began to revert to literary gossip.

Anna Bray sent her own latest novel, *Henry de Pomeroy*, which Caroline enjoyed and promised to send to Blackwood's suggesting it should be serialised in the magazine. She also read the *Diary of Madame D'Arbley*, whose half sister, Sarah Burney, had been a friend of hers in the giddy, Lymington days.

She greatly missed her outdoor life of gardening, walking and riding, all the more when surrounded by miles of dramatic and beautiful lakeland countryside. Short walks into the garden and field only made her long for Robert to be able to share it all, so she determined to get him a wheelchair. In July she wrote to John May, "I got him often out into the garden and field during the late glorious weather - in our borrowed apology for a wheelchair and it seemed to agree with him so well that I took measures to get a more commodious one of our own. Like many prudent people however, I was pennywise and pound foolish and thinking to get one cheaper here, I set a Keswick artificer to work - and the result of his skill, only just finished, was quite unusable. There was a description of one on sale at Bowness, but somebody made prize of it before I applied and now I have written to beg Dr Southey to purchase one in London and send it down by water carriage." A splendid new chair duly arrived.

With fine summer weather to help, Caroline was now able to spend some hours every day out of doors, pushing Robert round the garden or field with its wide view of encircling mountains, so that her own health and spirits much improved. In August the Burrard cousins arrived for a long stay. She had agonised for a long time as to whether they should be allowed to come to such a sad house, but they were determined, having been invited by Robert himself in happier days. They had nursed their own brother, Edward, through a long and fatal illness ten years before and were totally understanding. So August was a comparatively happy month, with cheerful company and frequent short outings along the lake. After so much sun and exercise Caroline felt almost able to face the rigours of the winter ahead.

Robert's physical health had obviously taken a serious turn for the worse since he could not now walk; mentally, he had been in a placid torpor, content to do nothing, but during the summer he had become more difficult.

"My dearest husband has been fluctuating - as to tranquility and excitement. Dr Irvine who sees him once a fortnight says his pulse is excellent - and there is no disease. But this must be all conjectural - and I have had some very uneasy impressions lately that the mischief does make progress." She went on to describe grindings of teeth, fits of rigidity and rolling of the eyes, which she feared showed increased pressure on the brain.

One of the thorns in her flesh, Cuthbert, was shortly to be removed. He was ordained on the 18th of July and then took up residence at Cockermouth where a church had been found for him. He had intended to marry also at this time, but this was delayed till the autumn as his fiancée had been taken ill. Bertha was occupied with two children of her own, one rather delicate. These were occasionally brought to see Robert - by their nursemaid.

Caroline still wrote to John May, one of Robert's oldest friends, dating from his youthful trip to Lisbon. He continued to take a warm interest in the affairs of Greta Hall and in one of his letters, inquires after Kate's health. Caroline is highly dismissive in her reply. "Kate's illness was months ago - a bilious disorder, nothing more. I heard of her constantly from Dr Irvine and he has long told me that nothing particular ails her now, beyond stomach derangement at times - and as she dines out whenever invited and is seen out every time, there cannot be much the matter - but she is not a healthy person - and would never I should think, under any circumstances have been in settled health of mind and body."

Later in the year the Hills moved to a large Elizabethan house in Warwick where Bertha's husband was to open a school. There was some discussion of whether Kate might join them, and Caroline must heartily have wished that this could be so, but remarked, "I have not the least expectation that Kate will ever go to her sister, except possibly for an infrequent visit. Her habits and associations and those of her old servant Betty are too firmly rooted to Keswick - and she will always prefer Cuthbert's vicinity to Bertha's. She is now staying at Cockermouth, helping to nurse her sister-in-law who is ill again - it was reported dangerously, but that cannot be, for Cuthbert came to Keswick the other day to purchase a horse, which he would not have done had she been seriously ill. He came also to look at his Father."

In other words, no one was allowed to be ill except Robert! It is remarkable how Caroline's own health stood up to the trials of these years and leads one to conclude that the semi-invalid existence she had led at Buckland Cottage must have been due in part to her loneliness and nervous state.

Family differences rumbled on and had repercussions even outside Greta Hall, with neighbours and friends taking sides. The Southey girls, Sara Coleridge and Dora Wordsworth had all grown up together, so it was natural for the Wordsworths to put Kate's happiness first and indeed offer her a refuge whenever she needed it. Caroline grumbled that William Wordsworth never came near his old friend, "except doing his utmost to misrepresent and injure his unhappy wife. He has passed through Keswick but never so much as sent an inquiry for Mr S to this house. He has been engaged I hear correcting the proofs of Dr Bell's life - the first part of which (my husband's) was by formal agreement with the Trustees - to have been sent to me for correction. I conclude that the intention is to violate this and all other conditions." This was unfair to Wordsworth, who had always looked upon Robert as an old friend. He kept away now out of a desire not to stir things up and indeed had spent a lot of time trying to reconcile the two sides.

In November, Dr Southey travelled up on a one day flying visit. Robert seemed not to recognise him all that day, but woke next morning crying, "Brother, brother," a heart-rending episode which strengthened Caroline in her belief that Robert could be mentally active if only he would make the effort.

With the new year she was torn between longing for the spring which had always been important to her own health, and might bring some change for the better in Robert's, and a desire for his death, that he might be at peace. Day after day, and night after night, Caroline nursed Robert. She was to look back and say, "Those three years at Greta Hall aged me more than twenty." Early in February, Robert took a turn for the worse. "Shaken I have been," she wrote to John May, "It was about nine o'clock on a Sunday morning that I perceived clammy symptoms. He was in bed in a deep, apoplectic slumber. So Dr Irvine found him when he came in a very short time - and decided on taking blood - three and a half pints - Even before the lancet touched his arm, however, he opened his eyes and smiled at me with evident recognition ... He has had a better night tonight. Well as he seemed the greater part of most days, his nights have been sadly distressing for two months past and more with convulsive agitation.

I do hope I may see him yet for a little while again completely calm and comfortable. While I say this I feel it almost sinful to feel comfort at the thought of his delayed blessedness."

Surely Robert's imminent death would bring the family together? But no. Caroline sent a message to Kate via the doctor and she came straight away to see her father and every day afterwards. She said there was something deathlike in her father's face which had not been there before and she looked to his release with agonised hope. She it was who summoned Cuthbert.

Worn out, in poor health, ground down by a hundred sleepless nights, Caroline concluded a letter, "My circumstances have in them the painful peculiarity of being made more distressing by the nearness of those who, in the order of nature, should be the fitting sharers of my troubles - I am isolated from all human sympathy in this place." But how much of this was her own fault?

Robert died on March 22nd and Caroline's long ordeal was over, though even death did not bring the two sides together, for Wordsworth was not invited to the funeral - he went anyway and later wrote the inscription for the Southey memorial in Crossthwaite Church -

> Ye vales and hills whose beauty hither drew
> The poet's steps, and fixed him here, on you
> His eyes have closed.
>
> His joys, his griefs, have vanished like a cloud
> From Skiddaw's top.

chapter nine

All here is finished, gloriously restored

At Greta Hall Caroline had known such brief happinesss with Robert, such years of suffering, bitterness, grinding routines of nursing and finally the deepest grief - one might expect her to fly off as soon as possible to the old sanctuary of Buckland. But she did not want to leave at all, had become used to the lofty rooms where mountains looked in at every window, the sloping gardens and the lakeside walks, and loved them still because they were part of Robert, all she had left except his books.

But it was far too big an establishment for one woman: though Robert had worked so hard and so long, his estate was not large, so the lease must be given up. In April, still under the hostile gaze of Cuthbert and Kate whenever they were visiting, she packed up her own belongings and sent her writing desk back to Buckland. Cuthbert was to be responsible for selling his father's library of twelve thousand books: Mr Taylor and the Trustees were to have charge of the literary estate. This was an added sadness for Caroline who alone had discussed his writing with him for the last twenty years: she felt, no doubt justly, that no one else was as well qualified as herself to see his last works through the press and understand what he would have wanted.

Even turned out of Greta Hall, she did not make straight for home, but went first to London to stay with Henry Southey in Harley Street. Henry had once remarked that his brother's mind must already have been clouded in judgement before he married Caroline, but he did not mean this unkindly, had always recognised the comfort and support she had brought Robert on his bereavement, and done his utmost to help her in the harsh years that followed, so it must have been a huge relief to be made warmly welcome by someone of Robert's family who shared her grief.

It slowly impinged upon her that there actually was a world outside the walls of Greta Hall. It had once been her pride to keep well informed of current affairs, politics and literary scandals to discuss with Robert: for the last two years she had known little outside - and it was an exciting place.

The great Whig reformers had finally been forced from office in 1841, to be replaced by the ministry of Sir Robert Peel. Income tax had just been brought in as a temporary measure, at sevenpence in the pound, and also the penny post. Iron ships were pioneering new ferry routes and a network of steam railways was spreading over England - the London to Southampton line was to open the following year. With the revolution in transport, ideas could spread faster. Whilst the nonconformist movement flourished, Newman's Anglo-Catholic fever was spreading through the intelligentsia. Darwin had returned from his expedition as botanist on the *Beagle* in 1836 and in 1839 had published his first book. James Simpson was experimenting with chloroform, which would revolutionise medicine for ever, and soon there would appear the first sparks of electricity - the mid-nineteenth century was a heady and challenging time.

Aching and exhausted, Caroline was hardly ready to cope with all this. From London she travelled on to Tarring and the Warters. This was the most healing thing she could have done, for it was not the hatred of Cuthbert, Bertha and Kate which had hurt her so much, as the fact that they were Robert's children. Edith-May had always taken the point of view that her father's last years would have been bleak and lonely without his second marriage, though of course her own marriage had removed her from the battle ground. She was genuinely fond of Caroline and welcomed her to the vicarage literally with open arms. Her husband was no less supportive, so this was a real haven for Caroline, a deep comfort to be held in affection by one of Robert's children. Edith-May continued what Henry Southey had begun, in building up her wrecked self-esteem.

Edith-May herself was not in good health: always prone to depression, she had been greatly shocked and saddened by her father's death, but she began to improve on Caroline's arrival and pressed her to stay on longer than intended. She stayed a fortnight, then insisted she must travel on to Buckland - not because she longed to reach her old home, but because seeing it was one more ordeal to be faced, as she explained to Anna Bray.

"My return to Buckland is a matter - not of choice, but of temporary expediency - for as my circumstances will not now permit me to reside there - I have only to look to the pains of re-entering the home he loved so much - without the prospect, which might be soothing, of taking up my future abode there.

But being at present unlet, it is a temporary refuge and I must be thankful to avail myself of it ... I cannot hurt myself to talk of Keswick and my last days at Greta Hall and my departure thence. Thankful it was - since to stay there was denied me - but when shall I cease to be there in spirit, though drawn thither by no loving tie?"

So in late spring, with the tall elms just coming into their tender green, Caroline came back to Buckland Cottage, after nearly four years away. The garden was overgrown; the rooms seemed small and dark after the lofty chambers of Greta Hall, but what memories crowded in, stately Grandmama in her Breton head-dress telling stories of the ancient château, her quiet father getting ready for a fishing expedition along the Boldre stream, the time alone with her lively, loving mother when they went gayly off to Lymington balls together, the long years alone with only Robert's letters as a lifeline - and Robert's visits when he had learned to love the cottage for its peacefulness. The memories of Robert were a two-edged sword now, but she would have been comforted by the return to her old home if it had appeared to offer a refuge for the rest of her life. Caroline was fifty seven.

Her annuity from Captain Bruce had ceased when she married Robert, who, with his own family to provide for, had only been able to leave her two thousand pounds in his will. In 1843 that was worth considerably more than it sounds today, since one could live comfortably on two hundred pounds a year, and the interest on her legacy would amount to roughly the same as the old annuity: nevertheless, Caroline entered Buckland on the assumption she must soon leave it again. Apparently it had even got into the papers that Caroline had been financially injured by her marriage into the Southey family. Edward Quillinan wrote to Henry Crabb Robinson, "On the contrary, she is two thousand pounds (that is the interest on that sum) the gainer by the connection, that being the amount settled on her for life by Mr Southey."

He then goes on to some wild, but intensely interesting statements. "An annuity which she received from as I understand it, the brother of some person to whom she was formerly engaged to be married, has lately ceased to be paid in consequence of the failure of the House that paid it - so far her income is lessened and it is given out, probably correctly that she cannot afford now to live in her own place in Hampshire."

Some of this is demonstrably untrue, Caroline's annuity having ceased on her marriage because it was no longer necessary. Can one give any weight to the rest then and take this as a clue that Caroline was once engaged to a Mr Bruce? Since he also refers to her as Catherine, it is difficult to place much reliance on the letter, though this the only name ever mentioned for the shadowy figure, Caroline's first fiancé.

Caroline continued to confide in Anna Bray. "If I can let my house, it must be early in next year. I need hardly say it is not possible for me to derive that benefit from the soothing influence of home which you kindly anticipated for me from my return to this place. But then again - is it not better ordered for me - now that my day is far spent, to have no abiding city here?" [She had written about her days being numbered twenty years ago!] "My broken spirit and listless temper would have made me fain to take up my abode here, had it been possible, for the rest of my days."

So she and Honor unpacked, and settled in, at least for that year, and outside the encircling trees, not far away, were old friends and family, the Rookes, the Burrard cousins at Walhampton and Edith-May not far away near Worthing.

Elsewhere though, feuding still split the Southey family. Edward Quillinan had recently met Kate in Keswick. "She looked very lovely and interesting, but she is a faded or rather blighted flower and the traces of severe suffering are but too apparent in her feeble frame and delicate countenance. She however seems happier than when her father was alive -and she is - as it were - only alive in him and his memory and all that concerns him and his literary remains. Mr Henry Taylor is collecting all the letters that he can of Southey to his various friends for future selection, and Kate, among others, is eager to give all the aid her recollections and knowledge of parties supply. One of Miss Fenwick's objects in going to Keswick was to try and soften Kate's mind toward reconcilliation with her sister Mrs Warter."

In particular, Henry Southey, one of Robert's executors, was caught between Caroline and the Warters on the one hand, and Kate with Cuthbert and Bertha on the other. Caroline was fully aware of his difficult situation. "Henry is so harrassed ... The distressing business of the executorship to his dear brother is peculiarly distressing to him. In consequence of those irreconcilable differences, he felt himself at least compelled to decide on - publish without reserve, and those who were on the spot so mismanaged the business, designedly as well as through their ignorance - that the loss to the other party will be very considerable. Through Mr Warter's kind and disinterested agency, a few relics have also been produced for me - such as I would not give, iron as I am now, for king's ransom. I am every day expecting my treasures - but they have to come round by Tarring. I shall not be able to resist unpacking them, though the sensible way would be to leave them ready packed against my next flitting."

Once reasonably settled, Caroline turned her attention to work. She did not yet feel able to produce anything original of her own, but was soon busy on Robert's. His three volume life of the educationist, Dr Bell, had been left unfinished: after much family wrangling, it was established that she should edit the first volume, while Cuthbert undertook books two and three. So she plunged into work - something she could still do for Robert (ironically this was just how Kate felt too) Letters went to and fro to Blackwood's. "I must have complete control."

She accused Dr Bell's servant of interpolating parts of his master's lectures into the manuscript. It was even necessary to correspond with Cuthbert, and various brief, business-like notes passed between them. To others, she complained how slow he was in his part of the undertaking.

In all fairness, Cuthbert had a new job, a new and delicate wife, and was busy packing up and selling the contents of Greta Hall, together with his father's vast library. Some of the books were sold by Kerslake in Bristol, the greater part auctioned in London. It must have been a very fraught time for him. Edward Quillinan went to the furniture sale. "On the late sale of Mr Southey's effects at Keswick I shall content myself for the present with saying that both Mr Hill [Bertha's husband] and young Southey conducted themselves like gentlemen, that everybody admired young Southey's demeanour and that I never in my life beheld so ill conditioned and unaccountably vulgar and violent and selfish a fellow as the vicar of ... he ought to be tarred and feathered. The sale I understand produced so much as thirteen hundred pounds. The books (chiefly rubbish for all the good ones are gone to London) sold at high prices. An interesting portrait of Chatterton I bought for Miss Fenwick." [A close friend of the Wordsworths]

By July, Caroline's need for money and a glimmer of hope that she might one day return to a creative mood caused her to write to Blackwood, "I do not say that I will never attempt to write again, for I should be glad to occupy my mind in any way that drew me from myself - but it seems to me now that I might as well try to make a watch go, of which the mainspring is broken. If you should please however to send me a retaining fee, I would try to make return." She added ingenuously that she ought not to expect a copy of Maga as well. So the rift with Blackwood's was healed. Caroline had been, after all, one of their most popular authors, with her work still being reprinted. They sent her a retaining fee each month and a copy of the magazine, which she welcomed as an old friend.

In the autumn she paid a visit to Wilton House, where the Herberts were an old family connection. Though she was still talking about letting Buckland Cottage for the summer of 1844, the final settlement of Robert's estate, her retainer and her royalties together made it possible to keep her old home and she was never to leave it again, except for social visits. Her last drawing of Robert, done in 1840 when he was staying with her, was framed and hung above her bedroom mantlepiece, where she might wake to it every morning. "You cannot think what a pleasure it is to me," she wrote to John May.

Since staying with the Warters on the way home, she had taken a keen interest in the vicarage household at Tarring, especially in the health of Edith who still suffered from depression and lived under the shadow of parents who had both lost their minds. Being bitterly sundered from her two sisters and brother could only worsen her state. She came to stay with Caroline and seemed to improve in spirits, but relapsed again at home. When Caroline went to stay at Tarring, Edith cheered up again, though not sufficiently to take over the care of her children, who were looked after by their father and the old nurse, Hannah. Edith-May was Caroline's one bright inheritance from her brief marriage and it was obviously good for her to have someone else's health to worry about.

In a long letter to John May she described Edith's health at some length. He like others was trying to bring the four young Southeys back together. "I should greatly regret you not having had the opportunity you wanted of seeing Kate and endeavouring to bring about a reconciliation, if I thought you had the slightest chance of success. But I do believe that whenever (for I will not say ever) a reconciliation can take place - it must be by way of Bertha - Fire and water will sooner amalgamate than Edith and Kate. They have tried what writing can do. It would be worse I believe if they were to meet. Edith would let out her whole heart - to be chilled and intimidated by Kate's self-possessed manner - well worded speeches and words that cut to the heart.

All this she smarted under during Kate's first and last visit to her in 1838. That visit, following upon Cuthbert's long domestication at the vicarage led to the pain of these unhappy feuds which were blown into active hostility by my union with their father.

Certainly all those persons who might have acted as peacemakers - and by God's blessing in some degree succeeded - took a very one sided, and therefore wrong view of the case. (I allude more particularly to the Wordsworths) and Edith deeply felt the falling off of her early friends, especially Miss Wordsworth, who had been to her as a sister." From this it would appear that Robert's marriage to Caroline was not after all the original cause of the family quarrel, but merely exacerbated it. Edith and the Warter family came to stay with Caroline in the summer. Edith always seemed to cheer up in her company.

By the summer of 1845, her own 'glass slipper of health' as she called it was sufficiently strong for her to go and stay with friends in Hampstead, from whence she went to dine with Henry Southey at Harley Street, hearing from him how some of the copyrights of Robert's work had been assigned. It was desperately important to her that all she had left of him, his work, should not suffer in any way: she was afraid that Cuthbert and Kate might in some way mutilate their father's work in order to popularise it and make more money.

She wrote to John May, "The Warters have got the *History of Portugal* and *The Doctor* - I am glad the first fell to their lot because it will be safe - not indirectly meddled with and brought to market. *The Doctor* I rejoice that they possess, not only because it is safe in that quarter but also, I think they will derive some pecuniary benefit from it. The whole business is painful, most painful, to me, and it sometimes seems to me as if it would disturb him where he is, if he could know how she is excluded from all participation of those treasures which he delighted to call hers - and over which he designed her to have control. The benefit in a worldly sense, you will give me credit for believing I care not a straw for - and whole heartedly rejoice that the four children derive much from the precious remains."

Caroline obviously felt that she should have had entire control of Robert's literary estate, though she was totally sincere in her remarks about money. She would have liked exclusive power to edit and publish, whilst passing on most of the money to his children. Money had never meant much to her as long as she could maintain Buckland Cottage. There was still the question of who should write the life of Robert and what should be done with his vast correspondence. It would have been far better had life and letters gone together, but owing to the family split, Cuthbert was to write his father's biography in six volumes and John Warter to edit the letters.

For all that Caroline was back among her old friends and family, it was most often news of the Southeys that filled her letters. Edith's children have a new governess who will keep them under control, for owing to Edith's poor health, they have been allowed to run wild. The Henry Southeys in Harley Street have a son Willy who is a sharp thorn in their side and oddly enough caught up in a situation parallel to Kate's, in that he disliked his step-mother and was intent on bringing his brother and sister to the same frame of mind. Cuthbert preaches a good sermon, though badly delivered, at Crossthwaite. In spite of all she had suffered, her thoughts were often there and in the Lakes. "Crossthwaite Church is now renovated and improved - is I am told, beautiful and Lough is decided at all regards to complete the monumental figure of my beloved husband in marble." This was a full length effigy of Robert, crafted in London, where she had been to see it.

There was news of Greta Hall too. "Our dear old house is at last taken over by a gentleman who has a large school and he is coming to it soon with all his train - it is well calculated for that purpose I think."

Her health fluctuated and for some time she was troubled, like Wordsworth, with sore eyes, but she had returned to some writing of her own and sent occasional poems to Blackwood's to justify her retainer. The one part of Robert's writings which remained hers alone, was *Robin Hood*, and she determined to finish this so that it could be published. Eventually it appeared in a volume with some shorter poems either by Robert or herself, each marked with initials. In this volume, love has blinded Caroline's literary judgement. Robert's mind was beginning to fail when they at last sat down to finish the poem begun so long ago - much better it had never seen print.

For the mid-nineteenth century it is very old-fashioned reading, as if the *Lyrical Ballads* had never been written. Robert's lines are desperately tired, with every adjective a cliché - good Father William, the innocent babe, the motherless innocent. Professor Dowden refers to it as a deformed child which should never have been brought to term. Caroline's own lines, about which she had been so diffident, shine out now and then, such as this description of a sunset, at the beginning of the poem -

> The long ranged windows of a noble hall
> Fling back the flamy splendour
> Wave upon wave below,
> Orange and green and gold,
> Russet and crimson,
> Like an embroidered zone, ancestral woods
> Close round.

Whatever its faults, the volume had given her great pleasure to finish and produce - the nearest she could ever come to working with Robert again. Also it must have salved her hurt pride a little, when the rest of the Southeys seemed to be busy editing Robert's work. The dedication read -

> Edith-May Warter
>
> Daughter and friend! My husband's daughter dear.
> Thou who hast been a very Ruth to me,
> Accept (to thee inscribed how lovingly)
> This wintry coronal.

Whatever the literary quality of the verse to follow, it meant a great deal to Edith to have her beloved father's last poems and her stepmother's affection bound together. Fortunately the volume attracted little critical interest for there were many new, more exciting writers on the literary scene by now. (Caroline actually wrote to Blackwood's to admonish them for not reviewing *Robin Hood*!) Alfred Tennyson had published three volumes of poetry, followed by *The Princess*, in 1847. Robert Browning was making a name for himself with his poetic dramas and innovative rhythms. Mathew Arnold's poems appeared in 1849. On a different plane but no less striking, Edward Lear's *Book of Nonsense* had been published in 1846.

Among prose writers, Harrison Ainsworth's last popular historical novel, *The Lancashire Witches* had just appeared, Ruskin was writing *Modern Painters* and Dickens was a household name with six novels to his credit including *Oliver Twist*, with *Dombey and Son* to follow in 1848. Women too were making their mark: Mrs Gaskell's *Mary Barton* was so graphic in its details of real life and labour in the north, that many found it 'disgusting.' In spite of Robert's initial dismissal of her gifts Charlotte Brontë's *Jane Eyre* was published in 1847 - what hope for success had poor, tired *Robin Hood*?

When she was well enough, Caroline put off the cares of editing, writing and worrying about the Southeys to work in her garden, pruning lilac and laburnum, dead-heading the roses, transplanting violets, weeding, sowing summer annuals, such as asters and mignonette, pottering about the winding paths, through the shrubberies and under the lime trees, clipping and watering

> ... employment sweet, for many an hour
> In tending every shrub and flower
> With still unwearied care.

And it was all her own - no one came to criticise, carp, or ignore.

Sometimes she rambled farther afield, up into the beechwood terraces of Buckland Rings, the hill fort close by, or down to the Lymington River where she had so loved to accompany her father.

Through hollow lanes and coppice paths,
By hill or hawthorn fence,
O'er thymy commons, clover fields
Where every step I take reveals
Some charm of sight or sense.

Since there was nothing more to be done for Robert, she now turned her attention to editing her own collected work. This was eventually published by Blackwood's and popular enough to be reprinted several times. Though called her collected poems, it did not contain *Ellen Fitzarthur* or *A Widow's Tale*, as they had recently been reprinted separately, or several long narrative poems which were to be found in the *Robin Hood* collection. There are ninety six pages of *The Birthday*, her finest work, and sixty six other poems, mostly short. The longer ones, such as *The Young Grey Head, The Evening Walk* and *The Broken Bridge* inevitably deal with tragic themes: those with enduring charm are most often the truly personal such as *My Garden*, (quoted above) *To the Sweet Scented Cyclamen* and *My Old Dog and I*

Apart from her prose stories, this volume was the crown of her life's work - and Robert was not there to read and appraise, but she was able to send a copy to Edith-May, knowing it would be received with great pleasure.

By the 1850's, Caroline's health had really begun to fail. She did not see very much of Henry Southey, but he had always been staunchly on her side in times of crisis and now applied to Queen Victoria on her behalf. A letter from Sir Robert Peel awarded her a state pension in 1852, which at least allayed her last fears of having to leave Buckland Cottage.

All these years she had kept up her correspondence with Anna Bray, always receiving replies 'warm from the heart.' Anna's novels based on the histories of Devon families, such as the Trelawneys and De Pomeroys were so popular that Longman's had recently reprinted them in ten volumes. In 1853 Caroline wrote to her, excusing her slowness in reply. "Every day since I heard from you I had hoped and tried - and every time fallen back upon the sofa pillows - fast asleep in a moment with the effort of arousing myself so far. Today I am no better but desperate - My cough gives me more respite in the evening and there is more life in me - thanks probably to a mutton chop and a glass of sherry."

For such a deeply religious woman, death had few qualms. As her health worsened, she must often have remembered how she and Robert had exchanged dreams of the after life, how they would visit distant stars together. She had faithful Honor to look after her and many who came to see her and offer help, but she really preferred to be alone. At last she was taken from the cottage to Calshot Castle and her much loved elderly Aunt Hannah. There she died in 1853.

"A few hours before she died she was watching a fine East Indiaman that had purposely run aground near the Needles Rocks, to avoid swamping a little fishing boat that had crossed her path. She observed to Lady Burrard, who was with her to the last, how impossible it was for her to realise that death was close at hand, with her mind so fully awake to the interests of life."

She was buried in the family grave in the churchyard of St Thomas, Lymington, once more surrounded by the beloved circle of her childhood, Mother, Father, Grandmother, Uncle Harry and many Burrard relations. But her last thoughts were surely of Robert. During the last few difficult years she had sometimes written poems, mostly sonnets, and one of these, perhaps one of her best, is her most fitting

We came together at life's eventide,

Fast friends of twenty years: cementing now

For brief duration here, with holiest vow

Our earthly union, sealed and sanctified

By an immortal hope. His mind would guide,

His strength support, methought, my feeble frame,

God strengthening both: in him the vital flame

Burnt up so brightly yet - so side by side,

Mutually comforting, we might descend

The downward way slow darkening, but than death

Worse darkness was at hand - more doleful end -

Not worst - not final. When with life's poor breath

All here is finished, gloriously restored,

Thee shall I meet, beloved, in likeness of thy Lord!

INDEX

Bath 37, 44, 52
Beaumont, Lady 80
Bell, Dr 100
Bentley, Elizabeth 105
Blackwood's 50-1, 69, 74-5, 85, 90, 95, 103, 106, 108, 119, 128, 133, 143-4, 148, 150
Boldre 4, 13-4, 30, 69, 117, 140
Bowles, Anne 1-7, 16, 32
Bowles, Charles 1-6
Bowles family 3, 22, 30
Bowles, William Lisle 52-3, 80, 109
Bray, Anna 99-100, 115, 122-4, 126-7, 131, 133, 140, 150
Bristol 36, 44-5, 48, 96, 101
Brontë, Charlotte 111, 149
Bruce, Captain 43-4, 74-5, 84, 108, 141
Buckland House 3
Buckland Rings 9, 30
Buckland, Waste of 9
Burrard family 6, 97, 118, 132, 134, 142
Burrard, George 28-9
Burrard, Hannah, Lady 72, 151
Burrard, Harry, Lieutenant General, Sir 6, 16, 19, 22, 24-5, 28
Burrard, Madeleine 6-8
Burrard-Neale, Harry, Admiral, Sir 6, 16, 19
Burton 95

Calshot Castle 6, 16, 19, 24-7, 30, 34, 106, 118, 151
Charles X of France 90
Cheam School 13
Chelsea 46-7

Coleridge, Samuel Taylor 15, 38-9, 52, 54-5, 119
Coleridge family 39-40, 55-6, 116, 130
Colling, Mary 99-100, 115
Cowes 91
Cowper, William 15, 107, 109-10, 112-3
Crabbe, George 15, 113
Darwin, Charles 139
Dickens, Charles 149
Dorchester, Lord 13
Dowden, Edward 86, 117, 147,
Durrell, Anne 7
Durrell, Madeleine 6, 28-9

East India Company 3

Fordingbridge 12, 94
Fricker family 37-8, 55

George III 6, 13, 19, 31, 44, 48-9, 61
Gilpin's Cottage 14,
Gilpin, William 13-4, 16, 113

Hill, Hubert 38
Howitt, Mary 97-9
Howitt, William 97-9, 107, 109

Isle of Wight 18, 24

Jersey 6, 8, 28, 86

Keswick 38-40, 54-7, 59, 64, 72, 80, 83, 89, 119, 130, 135, 140, 142

Lamb, Charles 38, 55, 61, 95
Longman's 41, 44, 49, 50
Longueville 8, 28-30

INDEX

Lovell, Robert 38
Lovell, Mary 39, 55, 119, 125
Lulworth Castle 91
Lovell, Mary 38, 55, 119, 125
Lymington 1, 3, 6, 13, 15, 18-20, 27, 30, 42, 90, 93 97, 133
Ma Bonne 7-9, 29, 34, 44, 72
May, John 129, 133, 135-6, 144-6
Murray, John 40-2, 44, 63, 89-90 92,
Murray, William 129
Myers, Rev. 131
Napolean 18
New Forest 1, 24-5, 30-1, 44, 60, 77, 95, 119
Newman, Cardinal 139
Newtown I.W. 92

Oxford 37

Peel, Sir Robert 92, 139, 150
Polignac, Princess de 90
Portsmouth 25, 97
Portugal 38-9, 72
Prince Regent 31

Queen Victoria 150
Quillinan, Edward 80, 125, 141-3

Robinson, Henry Crabb 117, 127, 131, 141
Rogers, Sarah 12
Rooke family 89, 97, 142
Routledge 51
Ryde, I.W. 91

Sadler, Thomas 102
Salisbury 31, 91

Scott, Walter 27, 40, 55, 63, 74, 95
Southampton 24, 30, 77, 81, 93, 101
Southey, Cuthbert 47, 55-6, 59-60, 84, 88, 109, 116, 119-121, 123-6, 130, 133-5, 139, 142-3, 145, 147
Southey, Edith 37-8, 47, 71, 79, 95, 101, 107-8, 110, 115
Southey, Edith-May 55-7, 101, 107-8, 110, 116, 124, 130, 132, 139-40, 142, 145-7, 148, 150
Southey, Dr Henry 129-30, 134, 136, 138, 142, 146-7, 150
Southey, Kate 55-6, 76, 116, 119-22, 124, 126-8, 130, 133, 135, 137, 139, 142, 145

Tarring, West 109-110
Taylor, Henry 132, 142

Walhampton 6, 13, 16, 19, 34, 51, 85, 118, 142
Warter, John Wood 101, 110, 124, 139, 143, 146
Weld family 91
Wellington, Duke of 92
White, Henry Kirke 34
Winchester 12, 69
Wordsworth, Dora 57, 98, 109, 125, 145
Wordsworth, Mary 127
Wordsworth, William 15, 27, 40, 55, 57-8, 80, 108-9, 112, 127, 129, 130, 137, 147
Worthing 142